Cosmic Fusion

Cosmic Fusion

The Inner Alchemy of
the Eight Forces

Mantak Chia

Destiny Books
Rochester, Vermont

Destiny Books
One Park Street
Rochester, Vermont 05767
www.DestinyBooks.com

Destiny Books is a division of Inner Traditions International

Originally published in Thailand in 2002 by Universal Tao Publications under the title *Cosmic Fusion: Fusion of the Eight Forces*

Library of Congress Cataloging-in-Publication Data

Chia, Mantak, 1944–
  Cosmic fusion : the inner alchemy of the eight forces / Mantak Chia.
      p. cm.
  Includes bibliographical references and index.
  ISBN-13: 978-1-59477-106-4 (pbk.)
  ISBN-10: 1-59477-106-5 (pbk.)
  1. Taoism. 2. Hygiene, Taoist. I. Title.
  BL1920.C2575 2007
  299.5'1444—dc22

                                                               2007007930

Printed and bound in India by Gopsons Papers Ltd.

10   9   8   7   6   5   4   3   2   1

Text design by Priscilla Baker
Text layout by Virginia Scott Bowman
This book was typeset in Jansen Text and Futura with Present and Diotima as the display typefaces

Contents

Acknowledgments

The Universal Tao Publications staff involved in the preparation and production of the first edition of this book extends its gratitude to the many generations of Taoist Masters who have passed on their special lineage, in the form of an unbroken oral transmission, over thousands of years. We thank Taoist Master I Yun (Yi Eng) for his openness in transmitting the formulas of Taoist Inner Alchemy.

We offer our eternal gratitude to our parents and teachers for their many gifts to us. Remembering them brings joy and satisfaction to our continued efforts in presenting the Universal Tao System. For their gifts, we offer our eternal gratitude and love. As always, their contribution has been crucial in presenting the concepts and techniques of the Universal Tao.

We wish to thank the thousands of unknown men and women of the Chinese healing arts who developed many of the methods and ideas presented in this book. We offer our gratitute to Master Lao Kang Wen for sharing his healing techniques.

We thank the many contributors essential to this book's final form: The editorial and production staff at Inner Traditions/Destiny Books for their efforts to clarify the text and produce a handsome new edition of the book, Victoria Sant'Ambrogio for her line edit of the new edition, and the artist, Juan Li, for the use of his beautiful and visionary paintings, illustrating Taoist esoteric practices.

For their assistance in producing the original edition of this book, we thank Lee J. Holden Jr. for his editorial work and writing contributions, as well as his ideas for the cover. We appreciate his research and great labor. We wish to thank Colin Campbell for his editorial contributions on the revised edition of this book, as well as thanking our Senior Instructors, Rene J. Narvarro and Annette Derksen, for their insightful contributions to the revised version. We thank Joost Kuitenbrouwer for his technical editing and clear writing throughout the book.

A special thanks goes to our Thai Production Team for their cover illustration and book design and layout: Raruen Keawapadung, Computer Graphics; Saysunee Yongyod, Photographer; Udon Jandee, Illustrator; and Saniem Chaisam, Production Designer.

Putting Cosmic Fusion into Practice

The practices described in this book have been used successfully for thousands of years by Taoists trained by personal instruction. Readers should not undertake the practice without receiving personal transmission and training from a certified instructor of the Universal Tao, since certain of these practices, if done improperly, may cause injury or result in health problems. This book is intended to supplement individual training by the Universal Tao and to serve as a reference guide for these practices. Anyone who undertakes these practices on the basis of this book alone, does so entirely at his or her own risk.

The meditations, practices, and techniques described herein are *not* intended to be used as an alternative or substitute for professional medical treatment and care. If any readers are suffering from illnesses based on mental or emotional disorders, an appropriate professional health care practitioner or therapist should be consulted. Such problems should be corrected before you start training.

Neither the Universal Tao nor its staff and instructors can be responsible for the consequences of any practice or misuse of the information contained in this book. If the reader undertakes any exercise without strictly following the instructions, notes, and warnings, the responsibility must lie solely with the reader.

This book does not attempt to give any medical diagnosis,

treatment, prescription, or remedial recommendation in relation to any human disease, ailment, suffering, or physical condition whatsoever.

The Universal Tao is not and cannot be responsible for the consequences of any practice or misuse of the information in this book. If the reader undertakes any exercise without strictly following the instructions, notes, and warnings, the responsibility must lie solely with the reader.

Cosmic Fusion and the Tao

Cosmic Fusion is the basic Taoist practice of Internal Alchemy. *Cosmic Fusion: The Inner Alchemy of the Eight Forces* is the second book in a three-part series. This book expands on the concepts and practices of Fusion I, which are introduced in *Fusion of the Five Elements*. Here, the practice goes to the next level of development.

In the beginning these practices may seem complex and mentally challenging; yet once the formulas are understood and applied, they are quite simple. With practice, the materials become familiar territory that you can traverse easily. Take your time with the formulas. Experiment with what works for you. The formulas are the guidelines to enhance your life. The Cosmic Fusion is a doorway into the vast potential of the self and the universe. It is a very natural process and the first step of the Taoist alchemical practice.

THE TAO

The word *Tao* means "the Way"—the way of nature and of the universe, or the path of natural reality. It also refers to a way in which we can open our minds to learn more about the world, our spiritual paths, and ourselves. Taoism is a practice of body, mind, and spirit, not just a philosophy of mind. When we have the true sense of the Tao, of its real

knowledge and wisdom, we will be able to make the right decisions in our lives.

Taoism involves many practical disciplines that can restore our lost youth, energy, and virtues while awakening our deepest spiritual potentials. Taoists regard these practices as a form of technology through which we can learn universal truths if we are willing to be receptive.

The ancient masters recognized that these potentials include the possibility of attaining conscious freedom and existence in the after-death state. Through specific exercises, the practitioner can avoid the suffering often associated with the experience of death by expanding the consciousness beyond the physical body before its demise. This makes it possible to determine one's future existence before leaving this life.

All spiritual paths ultimately lead to the truth. Taoism is both a philosophy and a technology for seeking and finding the truths of humanity, nature, and the universe. Its focus goes beyond one single path or viewpoint. Taoism is not a religion, as it requires no initiations or ceremonies; yet it is the outcome of all religions. Departing from dogma at the point of truth, it leaves behind all religious beliefs, like the clothing of past seasons. The goal of the Tao is also the goal of science; but the Tao leaves behind all scientific theories as partial and temporal descriptions of the integral truth. Taoism includes all matters of religion and science; yet its breadth goes far beyond the limits of devotion or intellect.

Taoist teachings are like master keys unlocking all doors. They assist people in their lives, as do all religious teachings. Yet the teachings of the Tao transcend religion while retaining the essence of spirituality. They explain and demonstrate the truths of the universe directly, rather than on the level of emotions, thoughts, or beliefs. For this reason, students of the Tao have little cause for skepticism or endless searching.

Philosophy, science, and religion all contain some aspects of the truth that comprises the Tao. The teachings of the Tao reflect the center of the ultimate truth (personal and universal) and help us reach it on our own. We can believe in any religion or spiritual path and still benefit from these teachings, because the Tao serves only to promote universal spiritual independence. There are no ultimate masters or gurus in Taoism because we become our own masters, capable of controlling our own destinies and knowing who we really are as we explore the marvelous powers hidden within the Tao of humanity. All the great gods, immortals, sages, saints, and holy men and women are our teachers and advisers.

Taoism, which dates back at least seven or eight thousand years, is closely aligned with modern technology and science. Today, much of the world's intellectual effort is directed toward external technological development. Browsing through a bookstore, you will find many current books that use the concepts of Taoism to explain relationships expounded by the "new" physics.

Thousands of years ago, the Taoists directed their consciousness inward and developed a science of inner alchemy. Each new dynasty saw the accumulation of more knowledge. Chinese written history has a 4,700-year span, and the language has not changed significantly over the centuries, so even the oldest documents can be read today. The Taoist sages, who learned and perfected methods to prepare and leave the body, recorded all the practical details. These, along with much that was written on philosophical thought, now fill the many volumes that constitute the Taoist canon.

Thus these transformative formulas endure as a gift from the original Taoist sages to all who are willing to put them into practice. The Universal Tao is concerned primarily with the practical approaches perfected by the Taoist sages.

THE UNIVERSAL TAO SYSTEM

The ancient Taoists saw the importance of working on all three levels of our being: the physical body, the energy body, and the spirit. All three are important in forming a ladder with which we may climb consciously into the spiritual worlds and, just as important, back into the physical world to be creatively active here. This ladder enables Taoists to learn about the inner worlds and to return to the physical with knowledge and increased energy. An immortal body, which is developed in the practice of Internal Alchemy, enables us to establish a constant link between life and the after-death (or prebirth) state.

The ancient Taoist sages believed we were born to be immortal. We become mortal by draining ourselves of chi through engaging in excessive sexual activity, indulging in negative emotions, and depending on material sources to supply our life force. The masters recognized that different levels of immortality can be achieved through internal alchemy, and they devised many practices for this purpose. The ability to transcend even death through the transmutation of our physicality into the immortal spirit body is the highest goal of Taoism. This level, known as physical immortality, takes the longest to achieve.

Healing the Physical Body: Becoming Like a Child to Return to the Original Source

Taoist practices teach us to conserve the physical energy so that it will no longer scatter and deplete as a result of our worldly interactions.

Full spiritual independence requires that we avoid being drained of this energy through the eyes, ears, nose, and mouth, or through excessive sex. The novice in the Taoist system begins with a wide range of exercises that develop the physical body into an efficient and healthy organism, able to live in the world and yet stay free of the tensions and stresses of daily life. He or she aspires to return to a childlike state of innocence and vitality, to regain the Original Source that is our birthright (fig 1.1). Specific goals at this level are to learn how to heal yourself, how to love yourself, and how to love others.

Fig. 1.1. Returning to the Original Source

On the first level of practice we develop a healthy body, and this can take months of diligent training. During this process we learn how to condense and conserve our life force through the Microcosmic Orbit meditation (see fig 1.2 on the following page), the Healing Love and Inner Smile practices, the Six Healing Sounds, and Iron Shirt Chi Kung. We learn to gather and refine our life force into a *chi ball* (energy sphere) so it will not dissipate when we are ready to leave this world. As people grow older, their life force weakens, often resulting in illness and suffering. Using drugs to combat illness drains so much of the body's life force that there may not be enough energy left to follow the primordial

Fig. 1.2. Uniting the heavenly force, the earth force,
and the cosmic particle force in the Microcosmic Orbit

light, the clear light, to the Wu Chi (our Original Source, or God) at the moment of death. The basic practices of the Universal Tao ensure that we retain enough of our health and vital energy to make that journey.

Stopping Energy Leakage through Conservation and Recycling

The Microcosmic Orbit is the body's major energy pathway. Along this path there are nine openings. If we learn how to seal them when they are not in use, that simple act of conservation will save an immense amount of energy.

The Microcosmic Orbit meditation is the first step toward attaining our goals, as it develops the power of the mind to control, conserve, recycle, transform, and direct *chi* (the Chinese term for energy, or life force) through the body's primary acupuncture channels. By learning how to manage our chi effectively, we gain better control over our lives; by using our energy wisely, we discover that we already have plentiful chi.

At this stage, the student also learns to connect with and draw from the unlimited source of universal love, a cosmic orgasm formed by the union of the three main sources of chi accessible to humans: the *universal* (or *heavenly*) *force*, the *earth force*, and the *higher self* (or *cosmic particle*) *force*. This process is both energizing and balancing. It prepares you for working with greater amounts of chi in the higher levels of meditative practice, particularly in developing the energy body.

Activating the Abdominal Brain

Learning to empty the mind is one of the most important Taoist practices. Letting go of judgments, suspicions, and the incessant repetitive thought process is a simple way to recharge the body, the brain, and the spirit. Science has shown that we have about sixty thousand thoughts per day and of those sixty thousand thoughts, 95 percent of them are the same thoughts we had yesterday. By activating the abdominal brain, we are able to clear the mind and create space for more creative mental activity (fig. 1.3).

The brain spends up to ten times more energy than the rest of the body. Even when we are not working or thinking consciously, our mind still wanders. In Taoism this incessant thinking is called the monkey mind. If we can stop the monkey mind and empty the

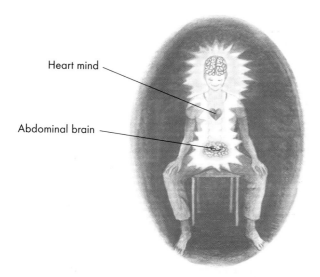

Heart mind

Abdominal brain

Fig. 1.3. Upper and lower brains

energy from the brain down to the organs, there will be a tremendous amount of energy stored in the body. This abundance of energy can later return to the brain. When the energy returns, our thoughts are much more refined, creative, and focused.

The abdominal brain is located in the lower tan tien, the reservoir of energy located about an inch below the navel and three inches inside the body.* This is the very center of our being. It is called the abdominal brain because it is a center for wisdom. Science is discovering that the same chemical activities that occur in the brain, occur also in the abdomen. The difference is that the abdomen is not connected with the senses. The senses tend to pull our energy and awareness outside of ourselves. This leads to the constant analyzing of situations and people. The abdominal brain is a much deeper sense of awareness, where our "gut feelings" originate. When the abdominal brain is activated, we open up to more guidance, deeper intuition, and full body awareness.

Transforming Negative Energy into Virtues: Opening the Heart

The Inner Smile and the Six Healing Sounds are simple yet powerful practices that teach us how to relax and heal the vital organs and how to transform negative emotions back into a rich source of energy. They help open the heart center and connect us with unlimited universal love, improving daily interactions and providing a vehicle for the virtues, which derive from the internal organs. Taoists perceive the heart as the seat of love, joy, and happiness, which can connect with universal love. It is also a cauldron in which the energies of our virtues are combined and strengthened. Through practice of the Inner Smile, you will feel these virtuous energies generated from their respective organs. You will then gather these virtues into the heart to be refined and blended into compassion, the highest of all virtues. This is a most effective way to enhance your best qualities (fig 1.4).

---

*These measurements are for an average-sized body and should be adjusted for practitioners who are smaller or larger than the average.

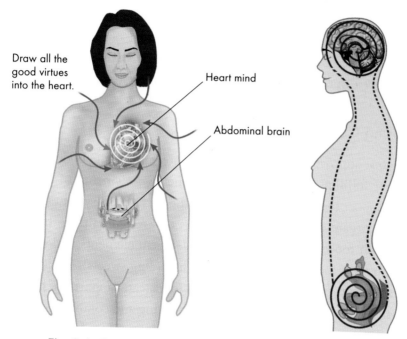

Draw all the good virtues into the heart.

Heart mind

Abdominal brain

Fig. 1.4. Conserving, recycling, and transforming the energy

Another important beginning practice teaches the student of the Tao how to gain strength through the conservation and recycling of sexual energy (see *Healing Love Through the Tao* [Destiny Books, 2005]). When collected, sexual energy *(ching chi)* becomes an incredible source of power that can be used by the individual or shared with a sexual partner via the Microcosmic Orbit pathway during sexual intercourse. With practice, singles and couples can learn to increase and intensify sexual pleasure. The collected and transformed sexual energy is an important alchemical catalyst to be used in the higher meditations.

Once you have an abundance of sexual energy, you can connect to the unlimited cosmic orgasm experienced every moment by your higher self, this being the most basic energy in every cell of your body.

Managing the Life Force

In the practices of Iron Shirt Chi Kung and Tai Chi Chi Kung, the student learns to align the skeletal structure with gravity to allow a smooth, strong flow of energy. With strong fasciae, tendons, and bone marrow and with good mechanical structure, we can manage our life force more efficiently. The body also gains a sense of being rooted deeply in the earth, so we can tap into the Mother Earth healing force.

Choosing Cosmic Nutrition

The Taoist approach to diet is based on determining the body's needs and then fulfilling them according to the five elements of nature, which support the five major organs of the body. This system reveals any weak organs and allows practitioners to strengthen them by balancing their food intake to enhance any deficient elements. It does not condemn most foods that people enjoy (including sweets), but instead creates a better program in which these foods can support the body's internal balance rather than disrupt it. Choosing and combining foods in this way can help us avoid the cravings we sometimes fall prey to.

Developing the Energy Body:
Our Vehicle to Travel in Inner and Outer Space

The next level of the Universal Tao system consists of the Fusion of Five Elements, Cosmic Fusion, and Fusion of the Psychic Channels practices. These practices build and enhance the Basic Universal Tao exercises (fig 1.5). They allow the student to use the extra energy saved through the foundation practices, including recycled negative energies, to build a strong energy body that will not dissipate. Developing this energy body awakens a part of yourself that perceives and acts free of environmental, educational, and karmic conditioning. Once the energy body is strong, it becomes a vehicle of great importance.

If we do not have a chance to practice awakening or to give birth to the soul and immortal spirit during life, the primordial light will awaken us at the moment of death. Unfortunately, we may be too untrained and inexperienced to follow this light. To prepare for the journey, we can train and educate the energy body to recognize and follow the primordial light, so it becomes a vehicle (like the space shuttle) to transport the untrained soul and spirit on the long journey home, back to the Wu Chi (fig. 1.6).

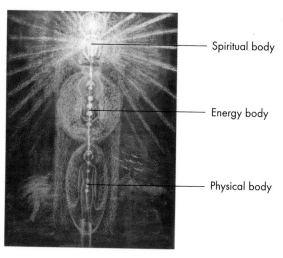

— Spiritual body

— Energy body

— Physical body

Fig. 1.5. Fusion is the first step in achieving union of our three bodies.

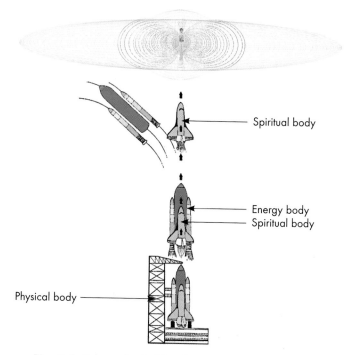

— Spiritual body

— Energy body
— Spiritual body

Physical body —

Fig. 1.6. Energy body blasting off the spiritual body
and entering outer space

When we are ready to give birth to the real soul, the energy body will act like a booster rocket to help boost the soul into its higher dimension of the immortal spirit. At the highest level, all three of these bodies merge into one.

Each level of development gives us a chance to go further in the journey back to the Wu Chi. Taoist methods of absorbing stellar energies help rejuvenate the physical body and strengthen the soul and spirit bodies for their interdimensional travels.

Recycling our Negative Emotions

Our emotional life, filled with its constant vicissitudes, drains our vital energy. Through the Fusion meditations, we learn to transform the sick or negative energy that has been locked up in the vital organs. Taoists understand morality and good deeds as the most direct path to self-healing and balance. To be good to others is good for ourselves as well: all the good energies we create are stored in the energy body, like deposits in a bank account. By helping others and offering them love, kindness, and gentleness, we receive positive energy in return. When we open our hearts, we are filled with love, joy, and happiness.

From Taoist experience, we know that when we leave this world we can go directly to heaven, depending on how much energy we have been able to transform into the energy body prior to death. Just like accumulating money in the bank, the more we transform our physical being to our spiritual being, the more we have in heaven. The more good we do here, the more positive energy we have up there.

Forming the Spirit Body from the Seed of Immortality— Lesser Kan and Li Enlightenment

The Inner Alchemy meditation of the Lesser Enlightenment Kan and Li (water and fire, multi-orgasmic sexual energy and compassion) reunites the male and female within each of us (fig. 1.7). It involves the practice of self-intercourse, which, through internal sexual coupling of the energies, enables the practitioner to give birth to the soul body (or

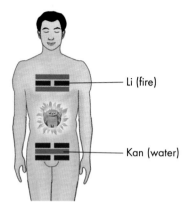

Fig. 1.7. Union of fire and water

Li (fire)

Kan (water)

energy body). The soul body then acts as a "babysitter" to help nurture the spirit body (fig. 1.8). The soul is the seed, but it can also mature into the immortal body if a person has not had the chance to raise the spirit body in this life. Practitioners of Taoist alchemy believe that if we give birth to the spirit body and develop the immortal body in this life, we can overcome the cycle of reincarnation.

Once the "babysitter" or soul body is formed, it is in the yin stage, a soul embryo or infancy. We need to feed, raise, educate, and train the young soul to become fully grown.

When the soul body is developed, we can give birth to the spirit body. To cultivate the young spirit body until it is fully mature can take fourteen to eighteen years. We also use the energies of nature (trees, sun, moon, and stars); virtually all sensory experiences of a positive

Fig. 1.8. Creating the energy body in preparation for the spiritual body

nature become nourishment for the growth of the spirit within the physical body.

Many masters who attained this level of the immortal body were able to transform the material into the immaterial and transfer it into the spirit body. At the moment of death, they were able to transfer their consciousness, their energy, and some of the physical elements of their bodies up with them into the spirit body (although even this level is not yet the true immortal body). In this process their physical bodies actually shrank in size; they may have weighed two-thirds of their former weight after their physical deaths occurred. This meant they had successfully transformed much of their material being into an immaterial state while retaining full consciousness.

Cultivating the Yang Stage, Marrying the Light— Greater Kan and Li Enlightenment

To merge with the light of the Tao, we must awaken and nourish the awareness that we are in truth children of the light. Once we have fully grown the spirit body, it will be the same frequency as the light of the Tao and can become one with it. We also refer to this light as the "outer light." Other traditions refer to it by such names as the Holy Spirit or Great Spirit.

The Greater Kan and Li meditation teaches us how to recognize the inner light of our own spirit and shows us how to merge with or "marry" it to the outer light (fig. 1.9). Once we connect with and "marry the light," we give birth to the second stage of the true immortal spirit. Taoists refer to this as the yang body. We continue to transform the physical body's energy to feed the immortal spirit so that it can mature.

At this stage of practice, we learn to digest increasingly finer energies of the higher self and universal forces from the sun, moon, planets, stars, and galaxies, and from the mind of the Tao itself (fig. 1.10). An awakening to that which is eternal and enduring occurs through this practice. Cognizant of our true nature as spirits, we experience the ability to leave the physical body and travel in the immortal spirit body, which leads to experience of the inner worlds of spirit. Fear of death is vanquished as we become familiar with life beyond physicality.

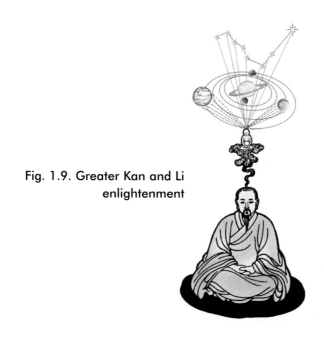

Fig. 1.9. Greater Kan and Li enlightenment

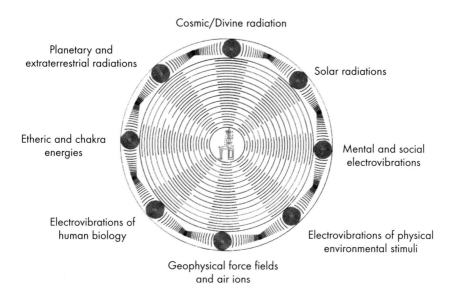

Fig. 1.10. Cosmic/Divine radiation fields

Manifesting the Rainbow Body— The Greatest Enlightenment of Kan and Li

At this level the practitioner transfers all physical essence into the immortal body. When all the body's material elements are transformed into subtle chi, what remains is known as the rainbow body. When a master of this level leaves this world, there is nothing left of the physical body but nails and hair. Death is still necessary to speed up the process.

Sealing the Five Senses, the Congress of Heaven and Earth, the Reunion of Heaven and Man

At this level, a master can transcend death entirely. He or she can simply transform the physical body into the immortal body and leave this world or return to it at will. This is the state of complete physical immortality. It takes from eighty to a few hundred years to complete this stage of practice and to transform all the material elements of the body into the immaterial. The final goal of ascending to heaven in broad daylight is reached.

There are records in Chinese history of thousands of Taoist immortals who reached the level of daylight ascension in the presence of many witnesses. In the Bible, Elijah and Moses also accomplished this feat. In the final stage of this practice, the adept can unite the immortal spirit body, the energy body, and the physical body, or separate them at will. It is then that the human being knows full and complete freedom as an immortal, and no world is a boundary.

Taoist Cosmology

Ancient Taoism is rooted in deep observation of naturally occurring universal processes and their effects upon human beings. Newtonian physics of the West understands these processes as the mechanics of cause and effect. Taoism understands them as the interactions of a vast sea of energy that is constantly creating and recreating the universe in infinite ways. Most religions and esoteric systems study these processes (the ways of God) through scriptures and practices based upon the immaterial. Taoism studies both the material and immaterial aspects of nature and the universe in the belief that the immaterial is both the source for the material and a product of it. In other words, physical and nonphysical processes are sources for each other (see fig. 2.1 on the following page).

THE VOID: OUR ORIGINAL SOURCE

Through observing nature and the effects of energy within the human body, the ancient Taoists were able to trace the universal energy back to its point of origin. Upon developing an empirical approach with which to contact this source of observable phenomena, they established the concept of the primordial void as the point of departure for all creation. This void, which was given the name Wu Chi, is depicted as an empty circle in traditional Taoist art because it is beyond human description. For energy to begin generating the effects and forms of nature and the universe, something had to stir within the Wu Chi.

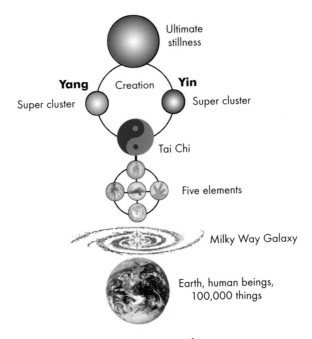

Fig. 2.1. Taoist cosmology

This first stirring created the division between the material and the immaterial, as all the processes of the universe began at this time.

Taoists refer to the first observable variations of the universal force, which emanates from the Wu Chi, as yin and yang (fig. 2.2). These two qualities of this force can be understood as the positive and negative poles of the primordial energy. Yin and yang are inseparable tendencies of all energy, and it is impossible to have one without the other. Their interactions are the root of all universal action; hence, the polarities of yin and Yang are an intrinsic factor of all creation.

The theory of yin and yang is expressed in a symbol—one of the most simple and sublime of all symbols—that illustrates the way

Fig. 2.2. The duality of yin and yang

nature and the universe interact. The circle that encompasses the symbol represents the Tao, the undifferentiated whole, the universe, ultimate reality. Yin and yang are terms that shed light on the process of the Tao. Yin describes the feminine, the contracting, the dark, deep side of nature, and yang describes the masculine, projective, electric, light, surface side of nature. Yin and yang are not two separate states, but an interwoven aspect of one. Just as day cannot exist without night, or male without female, yin and yang are opposite, co-existing elements of the same universal substance. They are the interwoven and continuous processes of decaying and becoming. Yin and yang describe a changing, dynamic picture of reality.

THE FIVE ELEMENTAL TENDENCIES OF THE UNIVERSE

The Taoists observed that yin and yang interactions follow five basic patterns that came to be known as the five tendencies, or the five processes of energy (fig. 2.3). (Such interactions have been misleadingly translated as five elements, thereby confusing the process with the actual physical elements.) In Taoism, the physical elements found in nature symbolically express the five tendencies of energy in motion.

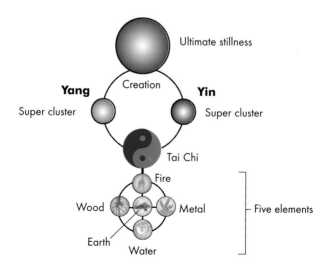

Fig. 2.3. Oneness, duality, and the five elements

Thus fire represents energy rising; water represents energy sinking; wood represents energy expanding; metal represents energy solidifying; and earth represents stable or centered energy. Each of the five elemental tendencies of energy are dependent upon the interactions of yin and yang emanating from the primordial void.

The five elemental forces are expressions of energy that can be observed in nature and throughout the universe. In space they influence the motions of all stars, planets, and cosmic phenomena. In nature they promote interactions between the five elements of fire, water, wood, metal, and earth. Within the human body they affect the five major organs of the heart, kidneys, liver, lungs, and spleen. Just as Western science understands the atoms and subatomic particles to be the fundamental units of all matter, the five elemental forces are understood to be the essence of all processes. The forces that influence the cosmos are identical to those that affect nature and our bodies. The Taoist understanding of the elements and correspondences in the human body allows us to transform lower into higher energies (fig. 2.4).

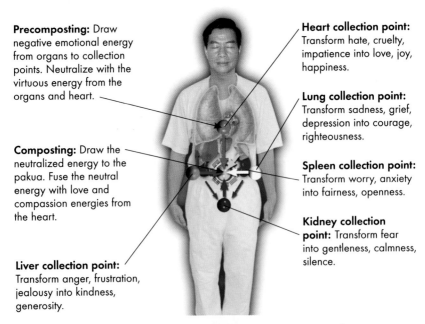

Precomposting: Draw negative emotional energy from organs to collection points. Neutralize with the virtuous energy from the organs and heart.

Composting: Draw the neutralized energy to the pakua. Fuse the neutral energy with love and compassion energies from the heart.

Liver collection point: Transform anger, frustration, jealousy into kindness, generosity.

Heart collection point: Transform hate, cruelty, impatience into love, joy, happiness.

Lung collection point: Transform sadness, grief, depression into courage, righteousness.

Spleen collection point: Transform worry, anxiety into fairness, openness.

Kidney collection point: Transform fear into gentleness, calmness, silence.

Fig. 2.4. Transform organ energies corresponding to the five elemental processes.

THE EIGHT FORCES

The eight forces represent a more detailed explication of the forces of nature and the universe. They are represented by the symbol of the pakua and the eight trigrams (fig. 2.5). In Fusion of the Five Elements,

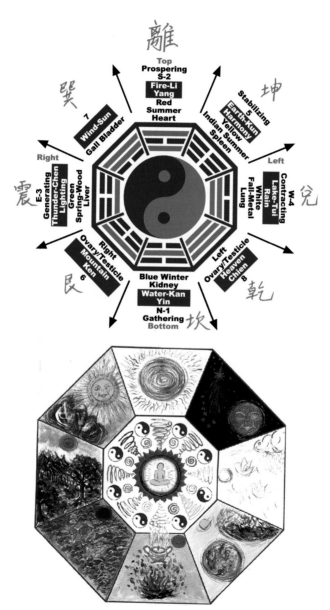

Fig. 2.5. The eight forces and directions

we began to utilize the pakua as a way to direct and gather the chi into a pearl at the lower abdomen. In Cosmic Fusion, we use the pakuas in greater detail, to create a stronger connection with the forces of nature and to draw much more energy into the pearl.

Using the pakua in the meditation practice is a way to focus energy. The pakua creates a vortex that enables the practitioner to collect, gather, and condense chi. This vortex of energy is used to not only create a strong connection within ourselves, but a harmonious relationship with all the forces of nature.

RETURN TO THE WU CHI

The Taoists realized that we are connected to the stars through our bodies, as the human form is a product of stellar energy and matter. With the basic understanding that human beings, nature, and the universe are all expressions of primordial energy (or the Wu Chi), the Taoists devised methods to tap the energy of the five elements. This was done to enhance the processes of the five elemental forces within our bodies, which can benefit our health, refine our spirits, and eventually reunite us with our source, the Wu Chi. Deep within our subconscious minds are memories and desires for the unity and bliss that preceded the dense vibrations of our gross physical state. So the ultimate purpose of Taoist practice is to return to our original state, the Wu Chi (fig. 2.6).

In the advanced disciplines of the Universal Tao, students begin to work more consciously with the five elemental forces emanating from the cosmos. Advanced practice involves collecting and absorbing energy from different sources in the universe while traveling in the energy and spirit bodies. Taoists move closer to the original source through the vastness of space in a similar way to a traveler moving from station to station in a train. Generations of Taoist masters have refined and mapped the simplest and safest approaches to follow. Because it is impossible to realize the Wu Chi in one step, we divide the journey into several stages.

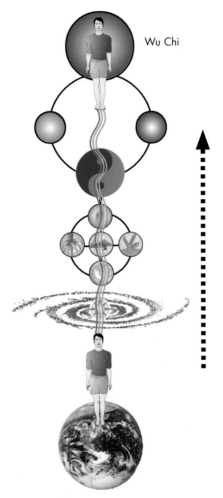

Wu Chi

Fig. 2.6. Return to the Oneness (Wu Chi).

1. The first step of stage one is to upgrade and maintain your physical health while stabilizing your financial and social conditions. Your body is a vehicle for processing energy, and the healthier you are, the more energy it will process at a faster rate. Your health and processing capabilities will improve greatly through the Microcosmic Orbit, Six Healing Sounds, Inner Smile, Healing Love, and Iron Shirt Chi Kung practices. Your finances and social interactions should be stable so that you can create space in your life for these disciplines.

2. Next you will learn how to use accumulated energies for traveling beyond this earthly plane to the moon, sun, and planets. This is similar to the way a space shuttle uses a booster rocket to push it beyond the earth's gravitational field. In Taoism the Microcosmic Orbit and Fusion practices create the energy body to help boost the immortal body (spiritual body) out of this world. The healthier you are internally, the more power you will be able to generate to leave the confines of the physical body. When you can travel out of this reality and back, you will gain the raw materials necessary to build more powerful energy and spirit bodies for longer and farther journeys.

3. The higher practices involve traveling to and from the stars and constellations, particularly the North Star and the Big Dipper, using the energy and spirit bodies. For Earth dwellers, the North Star is a stable and constant point in the sky. For Taoist practitioners, using the North Star was a way to find direction in the universe. The North Star is the gate of heaven. In the higher practices, the energy is drawn into the body to create that connection between the physical and the universal bodies.

The human body is a powerful transformer. The sexual energy is the body's most powerful source of fuel for journeys to the higher planes. This is why the Healing Love practice is so important for spiritual development. The practice of Iron Shirt Chi Kung also helps the physical body absorb cosmic energy through the skin and bones to be transformed and refined into more fuel. Fusion I provides another mode of energy refinement through the transformation of negative energies into positive life force, which is lighter and healthier for the body. All of these internal methods help us develop the means of traveling beyond this world. Their ultimate purpose (after rejuvenating the body) is to accumulate the raw materials for the construction of a stronger and more powerful vehicle for the return to the Wu Chi.

Many other systems have their own means of returning to the source. Monks, nuns, and priests emphasize detachment from the world and noninvolvement in worldly affairs. They have no intimate relationships with other people and no sex, which leaves them with abundant sexual energy to be transformed and used for higher spiritual work. Such spiritually inclined people make the best and most use of sexual energy. In general, when normal people accumulate sexual energy to the same degree as monks, nuns, or priests, they have no way to control it, and internal imbalances are created until that energy is released. The Taoist practices can give anyone the ability to use this energy to improve the body and spirit.

You should not believe in the Taoist teachings without experiencing the practice and its results firsthand. This involves learning about the human body, the universal forces that affect it, and the inherent desire we all have to return to our source. Taoism offers a clear, direct path to the Wu Chi, whereas many other systems provide only dogma and restrictions that can hinder spiritual growth. The Tao is not an escapist philosophy, however, as there is no need to remove yourself from society or restrict your relationships or sexual love. You can continue to live normally as you accumulate energies that will gradually improve your health while providing raw materials for the highest spiritual growth.

3

Goals of the Fusion Practice

The Taoist study of Internal Alchemy was introduced in *Fusion of the Five Elements*. The Taoists developed the Fusion of the Five Elements practice to intensify connections between and gain control of the inner and outer universes (fig. 3.1).

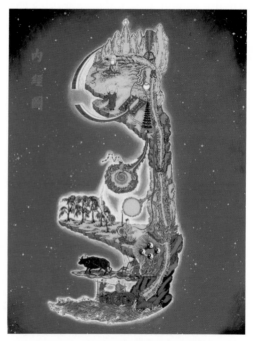

Fig. 3.1. Taoist Internal Alchemy

They understood that virtually everything that exists in the universe can be broken down into the five elements. The Fusion practice begins by understanding the dynamics of the universe, the planet Earth, and the human body with respect to their relationships to these five elements (fig 3.2).

Five planets

Fig. 3.2. The five elements, the planets, and the cosmos

The knowledge of Inner Alchemy is a necessary step in becoming connected to the outer universe, from which an unlimited supply of powerful energy is available to be used for an individual's physical and spiritual benefit.

The five basic formulas of Fusions I, II, and III can be likened to wiring blueprints for a spaceship, for making the subtle energy connections in the vehicle that link vital organs, glands, and senses so that their respective energies can be fused and balanced in the collection point and the pakua. The formulas lead the student systematically through the process of creating four pakuas and an energy pearl.

Table 1. Five Element Organ Correspondences

Yin organs	Liver	Heart	Spleen	Lungs	Kidneys
Yang organs	Gallbladder	Small intestine	Stomach, pancreas	Large intestine	Bladder
Openings	Eyes	Tongue	Mouth, lips	Nose	Ears
Positive emotions	Kindness, Generosity	Love, joy	Fairness, openness	Righteousness, courage	Gentleness
Negative emotions	Anger, envy, frustration	Hate, impatience	Worry, anxiety	Sadness, depression	Fear, stress
Transform pure organ energy into a virgin child dressed in	Green	Red	Yellow	White	Blue
Transform pure child energy into an animal	Green dragon	Pheasant, red bird	Phoenix, yellow on red	White tiger	Blue deer
Earth force takes the form of	Green dragon	Pheasant, red bird	Phoenix, yellow on red	White tiger	Black tortoise
Directions	East	South	Center	West	North
Planets	Jupiter	Mars	Saturn	Venus	Mercury
Universal energy force	Generating	Prospering	Stabilizing	Contracting	Gathering

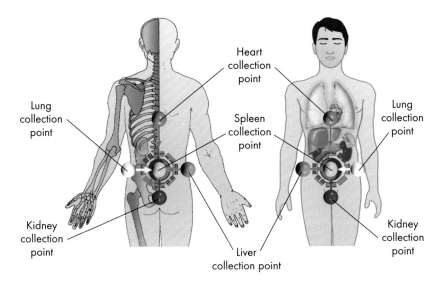

Fig. 3.3. Collection points

Energy drawn from the organs and senses into the collection points and transformed negative emotions are fused and condensed into a pearl through the pakuas (fig. 3.3). When the resulting pearl, with its refined, balanced, neutralized energy, circulates through the Microcosmic Orbit, the body absorbs this enhanced life force. The pearl is then used to form the energy body.

Cosmic Fusion practice builds on the foundation of Internal Alchemy laid in Fusion of the Five Elements. The student is encouraged to take this opportunity to review the basic Fusion practice.

Once the negative emotions have been drawn out and transformed, the pearl is moved through the Creation Cycle, nurturing the virtues. These qualities are cultivated, blended, and condensed into the pearl, forming the energy of compassion—the essence of the senses, glands, organs, and the mind.

The practitioner can now use this highly refined pearl to open and clear four of the eight specific energy channels in the subtle body: the three Thrusting Channels, used for cleansing and protection, and the Belt Channel, the protective belt route that surrounds the Thrusting Channels.

THE INNER UNIVERSE REFLECTS
THE OUTER UNIVERSE

The Fusion practice offers a practical way to strengthen the conscious connection with the outer universe. During the practice of Fusion, the essence of life force energy found in the organs, glands, and senses is transformed, purified, condensed, and combined with the universal force, the cosmic particle force, and the earth force in order to achieve internal balance. This transformation of quality energy into a harmonious whole can effect positive changes in the human body. Controlling this energy enables each individual to attain balance and harmony of these energies on physical, emotional, and spiritual levels. Because the inner universe is a reflection of the outer one, the balance and harmony attained in the inner universe enables the individual to attain balance and harmony with the outer universe. Fusion of the Five Elements focuses on the interaction and fusion of all five elements and their correspondences. To understand this interaction, especially with respect to the organs, glands, and senses of the human body, it helps to be aware of one of the Taoist laws of the universe: *Nothing remains the same; everything changes because the five energies of nature constantly interact and change.* This acknowledgment that change is constant contrasts sharply with the Western framework. Under this assumption, each individual's health and disposition are influenced by the inner balance of these five energies, a balance affected by the ever-changing conditions of the universe.

The outer universe comprises universal force, cosmic particle force, and earth force, from which all things emerge and whose three combined forces sustain all existence. The concept of Internal Alchemy is grounded in the Taoist belief that the inner universe is a reflection of the outer universe. There are connections that can be made between the inner and outer universe through which energy, recognized and experienced in the inner universe as chi, or life force, can be greatly increased and enhanced by the immense power of the outer universe.

THE UNIVERSAL TAO DIVIDES
FUSION INTO THREE PARTS

First Part

The Fusion of the Five Elements practice makes use of pakuas and energy collection points to balance, connect, and draw out negative emotional energies found in the organs. These energies, along with their corresponding glands and senses energies, are then fused and transformed into pure, life force energy.

The purity of this energy has an adhering and magnetizing quality enabling it to condense into a ball of refined energy which is called the pearl.

The pearl is then used to connect to the universal, cosmic particle, and earth forces whose energies become part of the pearl. A soul or energy body is formed from the pearl, enabling the individual to go beyond connecting with the forces of the universe on a purely physical level. Later the pearl returns to the organs and glands to enhance them, and provides a protection to the physical and soul body.

Second Part

Cosmic Fusion practice focuses on using the pearl to grow or intensify the energy of good virtue. It makes use of the interaction of the elements described as the controlling cycle or Creation Cycle of the Five Elements theory to circulate positive chi or virtuous energy through the major organs (see fig. 3.4 on the following page). All the energy gathered during this cycle is combined to form a beautiful pearl of compassion energy (see fig. 3.5 on the following page). This pearl is then used to open and cleanse specific channels that pass through the physical body into the energy body.

Third Part

The energy of the positive emotions of all the organs is absorbed into the pearl and then circulated in four of the eight special channels:

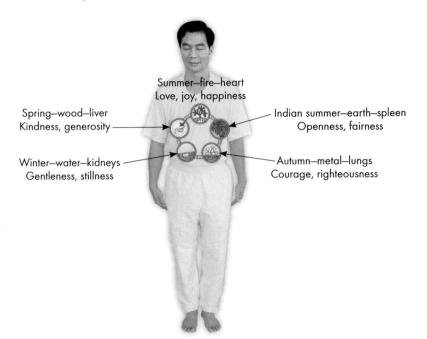

Summer—fire—heart
Love, joy, happiness

Spring—wood—liver
Kindness, generosity

Indian summer—earth—spleen
Openness, fairness

Winter—water—kidneys
Gentleness, stillness

Autumn—metal—lungs
Courage, righteousness

Fig. 3.4. The Creation Cycle in nature and in the human body

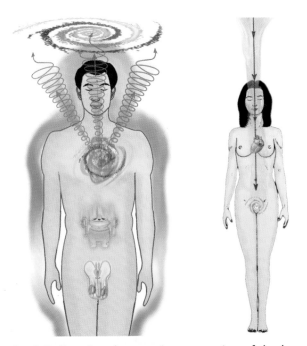

Fig. 3.5. Forming the cosmic compassion of the heart

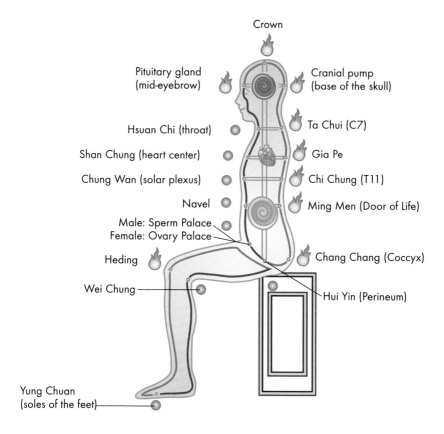

Crown

Pituitary gland
(mid-eyebrow)

Cranial pump
(base of the skull)

Hsuan Chi (throat)

Ta Chui (C7)

Shan Chung (heart center)

Gia Pe

Chung Wan (solar plexus)

Chi Chung (T11)

Navel

Ming Men (Door of Life)

Male: Sperm Palace
Female: Ovary Palace

Heding

Chang Chang (Coccyx)

Wei Chung

Hui Yin (Perineum)

Yung Chuan
(soles of the feet)

**Fig. 3.6. The Microcosmic Orbit with
ancient Chinese points noted**

the Microcosmic Orbit (Governor and Functional Channels) (see fig.
3.6), the Thrusting Channels (or Routes), and the Belt Channels (or
Routes). The Thrusting Channels run vertically through the center
of the body, linking the chakra centers (see fig. 3.7 on the following page). The Belt Channels spiral horizontally around the body,
strengthening the aura and providing a form of psychic self-defense
(fig. 3.8 on the following page).

The three Thrusting Channels, and the Belt Channels, which
the practitioner opens during Cosmic Fusion, permit a freer flow of
energy throughout the body.

The Thrusting Channels are opened first. Their primary function
is to cleanse specific energy pathways in the body, thereby opening

them up for the energy to flow freely. The Belt Channels surround the physical body and the internal Thrusting Channels. Both routes help to build a denser body and provide protection to the body, but they have higher function as well.

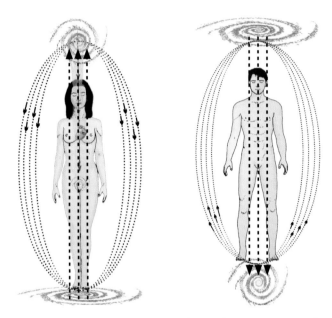

Fig. 3.7. The Cosmic Thrusting Channels in women and men

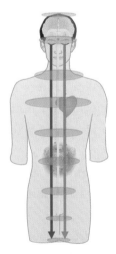

Fig. 3.8. The Belt Channels

With the additional energy generated during the practice of Fusion II, you will have enough energy to create a new energy body above the physical body. Another important aspect of the Fusion of the Five Elements practice is learning how to temporarily separate the energy body and the physical body. In life, our three bodies, the physical body, energy body, and spirit body (consciousness), all overlap and are generally inseparable. At death, the physical body is no longer a fit vehicle for holding the material five elements together, and chi and consciousness are forced to leave. To avoid the traumatic disorientation and confusion that can occur at death when the energetic essence and consciousness are involuntarily thrust out of the physical body into unknown territory, we can familiarize ourselves with the "out-of-body realm" by temporarily separating the energy body and spiritual body from the physical body, as a "dress rehearsal" for death.

Consciousness always requires some sort of vehicle in order to manifest. Its gross vehicle is the physical body. Its more subtle vehicle is the energy body (sometimes referred to as the subtle body). We emphasized earlier that the virtues are the true energetic essence of our organs. Although we may identify ourselves more with our physical body than anything else in the world, it is our energetic essence, not our physical body, that survives after death and has the capacity to be immortal.

The Thrusting Channels and Belt Channels can be extended up into this energy body and spiritual body. In this way they serve as connecting links between the organs and glands of the physical body and the transferred consciousness that is the energy body. Eventually, the channels serve as conduits through which the spirit body is boosted to the Mid-Plane. These advanced practices are called the meditations of Kan and Li.

If you think of the energy body as a booster rocket, then the spirit body would be the shuttle (see fig. 3.9 on the following page). Once the spirit body is boosted through the open channels into the Mid-Plane, it collects a higher quality of energy. The spirit body then returns with the higher-quality energy to the physical body. In the next effort this energy

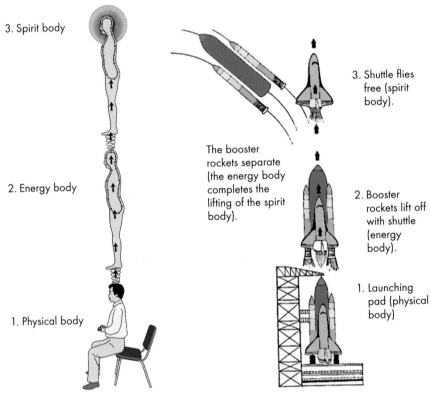

Fig. 3.9. The physical, energy, and spiritual bodies

is used to construct a stronger, more intense energy body that can boost the spirit body to a higher Mid-Plane level. The cycle continues, bringing the spirit body to higher and higher levels, while increasing the life force energy for use by the physical, energy, and spirit bodies.

By regularly turning our awareness inward in the Fusion of the Five Elements practice, we gradually come to know our energetic essences as well as we know our face, our arms, and our legs. We learn to distill these essences into a pearl, as a sort of space capsule to carry our essential energy and consciousness out of the physical body. With regular practice, Taoists who follow the path of Internal Alchemy learn to move their energy body and consciousness in and out of their physical body as easily as one might walk from one room into another.

Energetic Preparations for Meditation Practice

Meditation practices are enhanced by developing our sensitivity to subtle energy and by exercising to improve postural alignment, increase flexibility of the spine, and deepen relaxation of the physical body. This chapter presents a series of suggested exercises to help students meet these goals.

Chi generates many sensations. Some of the most common are tingling, heat, expansion, electrical sensations (like the feeling of static electricity), pulsation, and effervescence. These are not the actual chi itself, but the signs of increasing chi in a particular area. Chi itself is more mysterious, subtle beyond definition. For more details on chi in the practices of Spinal Cord Breathing, Rocking the Spine, and the Inner Smile to relax the whole body, refer to the Universal Tao book *Awaken Healing Light of the Tao*.

PREPARING FOR THE FUSION MEDITATIONS

Prepare the Environment

Find a quiet place to meditate where there are no distractions. Some places have naturally peaceful chi: mountains, forests, caves, gardens, monasteries, or beautifully designed meditation rooms. Once you have experienced such a place, you can recall it whenever you want to. Set aside a corner of your room for your practice, and recall your connection to the forces of nature.

Keep your meditation place clean and pleasant. Avoid interruptions by planning. Plan to meditate early in the morning before other people are awake: the body is rested, the air is fresh, and the earth itself is energized. Late at night is also fine. Select a time that works well for you with your own rhythms and schedule. If you create the space and allow yourself the time each day to cleanse your emotional, energetic, and physical bodies, you will soon reap the rewards in every area of your life.

Conserve Energy and Purify Your Body with an Appropriate Diet

To clear your digestive tract, it helps to reduce the total amount you eat, to eat less meat, fish, and poultry, and to increase the amount of fiber in your diet. Unless you are a vegetarian, it is recommended that you eat about 80 percent grains and vegetables, 10 to 15 percent fish, and only 5 percent meat and chicken.

Loosen, Stretch, and Warm Up the Body before Meditating

Once you have a quiet place and are ready to meditate, spend time loosening up the body, particularly the spine, before you sit down to practice.

The Universal Tao recommends doing some stretching exercises, Chi Kung, and Tai Chi before you begin to meditate. These exercises are both invigorating and relaxing; they relieve muscle tensions, stimulate the blood circulation, get rid of stale air in the lungs, and oxygenate the blood. As an alternative, you can take a relaxing stroll outdoors.

Doing some movement before entering the stillness of meditation can help you shake off the sluggishness that comes from being too sedentary and ease the tensions that might build up during a hectic day. Then when you sit down, you are truly ready to begin. Use the Simple Chi Kung exercises to loosen your spine and prepare the mind and body for meditation.

Wear Loose and Comfortable Clothing

The clothing you wear for meditation should be loose and comfortable. It is very important that your clothes restrict neither the chi flow, the blood circulation, the nervous system, nor the breath.

It is preferable to wear clothing of natural fibers so your body can breathe. During meditation, all the pores open wider, and breathing in energy through them requires looser clothing. When you have learned to breathe through the skin, your body will need to contact more fresh air.

ESTABLISH A STABLE SITTING POSITION

The body must be stable for the mind to be stable. It has been said, "An anxious mind cannot exist in a relaxed body." The mind and body are clearly connected, and when the body and breath become peaceful, the mind easily follows.

If your posture is firm and balanced, it will be easy for you to relax, and you will already be halfway toward achieving a tranquil and focused mind. But if your posture lacks balance and stability, your muscles will soon tire and become tense, and your attention will waver like a candle in the wind.

Consider these seven points in preparing a good meditation posture: base, hands, spine, shoulders, chin, eyes, and tongue.

Base

Your base is the foundation of a good meditation posture. To accommodate the movement of internal and external forces we generate when doing the Taoist practices, we need to stay grounded and establish a good connection with the earth's energy. The more chi that moves through the body, the more important grounding becomes, to prevent overheating of the organs and other negative side effects.

The soles of the feet provide an ideal connection to the earth through the Yung Chuan (Bubbling Spring) points. These are specifically designed to absorb the earth's energy and conduct it up into the body. The legs also help filter the raw energy to make it more readily digestible.

It is best to sit on a straight-backed chair to practice the Fusion meditations. Your weight should be evenly divided over four points: your two feet and the two sitz bones (the tuberosities of the ischium) (fig. 4.1). Place the feet flat on the floor the same distance apart as the hips. The calves of the legs should be vertical, like pillars. Try to have the knees and hips at the same level, or keep the knees slightly higher.

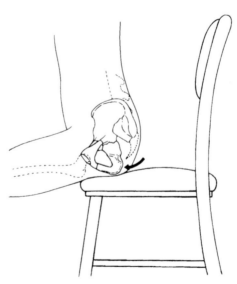

Fig. 4.1. The sitz bones

The part of the pelvis known as the ischium is structurally designed to hold a tremendous amount of weight. Avoid leaning back and sitting on the coccyx and sacrum instead of the ischium. Honor Mother Nature's design by sitting on the ischium and not on the tailbone, which puts pressure on the sacrum, one of the major pumps in the spine for cerebrospinal fluid, a vital cushion for the nervous system. Check to make sure your weight is evenly distributed over the four points to establish a solid base to support the body during meditation.

Hands

Let your hands rest in your lap, clasped lightly together with the right palm over the left palm and the right thumb and forefinger wrapped around the base of the left thumb. You may rest your hands on a pillow placed on your lap (fig. 4.2). The clasped hand position works especially well to consolidate and balance the energies generated during the meditation.

Fig. 4.2. Using a small pillow helps release shoulder stress.

Spine

The spine should be straight but not stiff, and in good vertical alignment with gravity. You can imagine your head being pulled up by a string. As it rises, allow the spine to elongate, increasing the space between vertebrae (fig. 4.3).

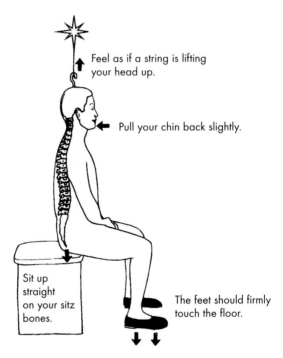

Feel as if a string is lifting your head up.

Pull your chin back slightly.

Sit up straight on your sitz bones.

The feet should firmly touch the floor.

Fig. 4.3. The correct sitting position

Some people find that their backs become tired during long rounds of meditation. Good alignment helps prevent this by taking some of the stress off the muscles and putting it instead on the skeletal structure where it belongs. The skeletal structure is designed to support hundreds of pounds without effort when properly aligned. Practicing Iron Shirt Chi Kung and Tai Chi is very helpful for strengthening the muscles you use in sitting and for learning the body mechanics of good alignment.

The spinal column houses many nerves, and it is also a major part of the Microcosmic Orbit pathway. If the spine feels relaxed, clear, and open, the mind will feel more awake and alert too.

Shoulders

The shoulders should be relaxed and balanced over the hips. The arm-pits should be slightly open, allowing enough space to hold a Ping-Pong ball (fig. 4.4). This permits free circulation of blood and chi into the arms and keeps the nerves in the arms from being impinged.

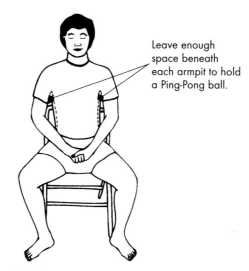

Leave enough space beneath each armpit to hold a Ping-Pong ball.

Fig. 4.4. The correct arm position

Chin

The chin should be drawn back slightly, with as little strain as possible, so that the ears are over the shoulders. If you strain too much to bring the head back, your muscles will soon tire.

Eyes

Your eyes should generally be closed or slightly open with the gaze directed downward. Or you can focus on the nose, and from the nose focus into the heart. You can open your eyes for a while if you feel sleepy or distracted (see fig. 4.5 on the following page).

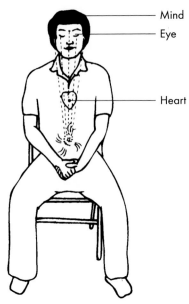

Fig. 4.5. Turn the mind and eyes inward. Focus into the
heart and then down into the navel.

Tongue

The tip of the tongue should be touching the upper palate (fig. 4.6).
This connection acts like a switch in that it connects the Tu Mo and
Ren Mo, the Governor and Functional Channels. The best point for
you to use is the one where you feel the strongest sensation of chi.

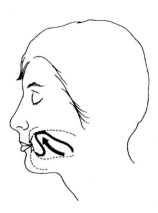

Fig. 4.6. Touch the tip of your tongue against the upper palate.

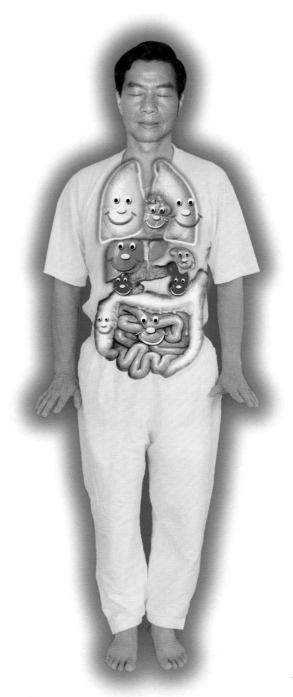

Fig. 4.7. Smile to the organs and feel the
organs smile back to you.

Beginning Fusion Element Meditation

THE PAKUA

The pakua is a symbol of the eight natural forces of the universe. The word *pa* means "eight"; *kua* means "trigram." The symbol is a three-dimensional octagon of eight trigrams with the Tai Chi (or yin/yang) symbol in the center, which spirals to blend and transform the energies (fig. 5.1). Forming of the pakuas is used in all the Fusion formulas. In the Fusion of the Five Elements meditation, we use the pakuas

Fig. 5.1. The pakua—a symbol of the eight forces

to gather and collect the energy of the organs and fuse them into a pearl. Here in the Cosmic Fusion meditation, we again use the pakuas to fuse energy into a pearl. Now, instead of just using the energy within the body, we combine the energy of the organs with the energy of the universe. We do this by using the Fusion practice to gather and condense the abundant energy that surrounds us into something that is usable and digestible to the body.

The first step is to form the pakua at the lower abdomen, to connect with and attract the five energies and the eight forces. The goal is to balance and transform the emotional energies of the organs. The next step is to form the facial pakua. The facial pakua gathers and transforms the energy of the senses and the thoughts and collects them in the lower abdomen. The next step is to create the universal pakua to gather and collect the energy of the universe into the lower abdomen. All these energies, once gathered, are condensed into an energy ball, or a pearl of white light. This highly refined ball of energy is then circulated through all the channels as a way to open, heal, and revitalize the body, mind, and spirit. This is the beginning of the transference of consciousness to a new realm.

CHANTING

Chanting has been used in all systems of spirituality to help connect practitioners to their higher source. In Christianity, chanting and singing is used to connect with God. In Buddhism and Hinduism, chanting is used to clear the space, to open the body, and to connect with the Buddha or a Hindu god or goddess. We can see the power of chanting and singing not only in religious settings, but in all levels of society as well. Singing and listening to music is a very natural way to move energy.

In the Taoist practice, we use chanting to invoke the forces of the universe. This is not necessarily about harmony. We want to get depth and power to the vibration, to open the lower abdomen and create internal power. When you chant, you should try to feel the vibration coming from the lower tan tien.

Chanting in the pakua is very similar to the sound in the genes when the replicating strands of DNA cross over. The eight sounds are the songs of the crossing of the chromosomes, like two serpents who entwine and make love, and then one becomes two. The metaphorical images we make use of to consciously enhance the movement of energy have much in agreement with the evidence of modern genetic science, as witnessed by two recent books, *DNA and the I Ching*, by Johnson F. Yan, and *The I Ching and the Genetic Code*, by Dr. Martin Schönberger.* Science puts the images in terms of biochemicals and energy frequencies, but the descriptions are congruent.

The pakua is a symbolic representation of the forces that exist in nature. By chanting the name of each force, you are able to make a connection with that force. Also, chanting yin and yang is a way to contract and expand energy. The combination of chanting the forces and chanting yin and yang helps to bring the power of the universe to you.

Chanting greatly increases the power and the coherence of the pearl. After you have toned all eight directions, the forces of the universe are fused into the pearl. The yin and yang (Tai Chi spines) chanting helps to expand and gather, as well as to contract and store, the force. This, in turn, helps create the connection between your internal energy and the energy of the universe.

Note: Chanting with others in a group makes the chanting much more powerful.

FORMULA ONE: FORMING THE PAKUAS

There are two arrangements of the pakuas: the Earlier Heaven and the Later Heaven (fig. 5.2). It is said that the Earlier Heaven pakua was revealed to Fu Hsi, a legendary figure of early Taoist history; some say it was inscribed on a horse, others say on a dragon that rose from

---

*Johnson F. Yan, *DNA and the I Ching* (Berkeley, Calif: North Atlantic Books, 1991); and Dr. Martin Schönberger, *The I Ching and the Genetic Code* (Santa Fe, N.M.: Aurora Press, 1992).

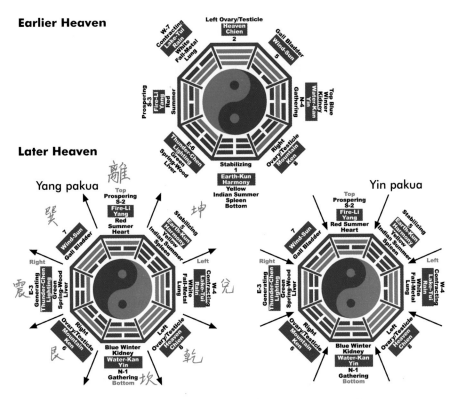

Fig. 5.2. The Earlier Heaven and Later Heaven pakuas

the river Ho as the Ho-tu. The Later Heaven pakua was revealed to another legendary king, Yỡ the Great, as the Lo-shu; this time it was written on the shell (back) of a tortoise that emerged from the river Lo. The Earlier Heaven pakua shows the unchanging cycle of these energies, the natural order of the universe, and is the foundation of Fu Hsi's divinational trigrams/hexagrams, making up the I Ching. The Later Heaven pakua shows the opposing interaction of these energies, which are responsible for the changes and creation of all the things in the universe, in nature, and in our own lives.

 Creating the Front Pakua: The First Four Trigrams

It is important to become familiar with the pakua and comfortable visualizing it. Training the mind to concentrate on a single image is of immeasurable value for spiritual practice. The image of the pakua allows the mind to focus and fuse energy. This first step is essential to the whole Fusion practice. One of the best ways to get this image deeply established in your mind is to draw it on a piece of paper and place it over your abdomen. Or, if you are a little more adventurous, draw it directly on the abdomen. When you draw the pakua, use blue for yin, red for yang and black for the frame. Sometimes it helps to work with a partner. Draw the pakua over your partner's abdomen, and do the meditation facing each other. This way you can glance at the pakua and know what forces to work with. Be creative. Do whatever works so that you get the image planted firmly in your mind.

Form the pakua below the underside of the rib cage and above the top of the pubic bone. When chanting the symbols of the trigrams, you can use your finger to draw them on your own abdomen, or find them on the pakua on your partner's abdomen.

There are three major centers for generating the energy frequency that is the main energy of the body (fig. 5.3):

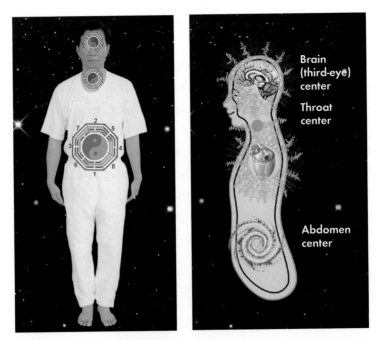

Fig. 5.3. Three energy centers

1. Tan tien (the main chi center, where chi can be measured like heat in infrared rays)
2. Throat center
3. Third-eye center

 *Kan: The First Sound*

Kan (yin yang yin) is the power symbol of the element water, the gathering yin power, connected with the kidneys, ears, and sexual organs. You will evoke the energy of the symbol by repeating its sound, *kan, kan, kan*, several times, or until you feel the connection with the energy of kan, spreading down to the sexual organs and the kidneys (fig. 5.4). The kan sound should come from the abdomen and the throat.

1. **Chant kan:** First chant the name of the trigram kan in a long and deep sound while you picture the symbol and touch your lower abdomen. Your eyes look downward to the lower abdominal area.
2. **Chant the trigram:** Next, chant the yin and yang lines of the symbol one after the other, *yin yang yin, yin yang yin*. Always start from the inner side, close to the Tai Chi symbol.

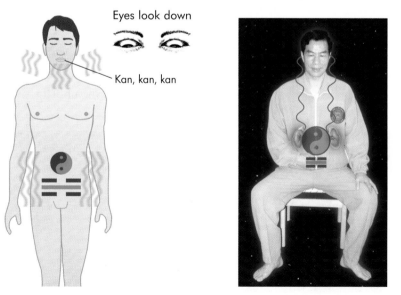

Fig. 5.4. Chant *kan* (ears and kidneys connect to the kan).

3. **First line, yin contraction**: Focus on the innermost yin line. Start with the mind expanded and the hands and palms expanded to touch the universe, the cosmos. Chant the *yin, yin, yin* as long as you feel comfortable, and move your palms to draw the cosmic chi from the universe into the navel. Feel that the navel has suction. Feel your hands and the tan tien; the throat has the power to suck the chi down to the yin line at the navel. Rest (fig. 5.5).

Fig. 5.5. Yin line: contract

4. **Middle line, yang expansion:** Be aware of the tan tien, throat, and crown. Hold the palms close to the navel and slowly chant the long yang sound. Turn the palms out, and gradually move the hands outward to the left and right sides. Feel your palms very long and big, reaching out, touching the cosmos. Rest in this expanded position, and feel your palms in touch with the cosmic chi (fig. 5.6).

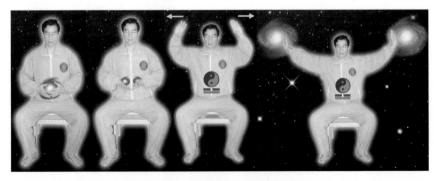

Fig. 5.6. Yang line: expand

5. **Last line, yin contraction:** With the mind, the hands, and the palms expanded to touch the universe, chant the *yin, yin, yin* as long as you feel comfortable, and continue moving your palms to draw the cosmic chi from the universe into the navel. Feel the navel has suction. Feel your hands and the tan tien; the throat has the power to suck the chi down to the yin line at the navel. Rest for a while. Feel the vibrations inside as you chant the trigram (fig. 5.7).

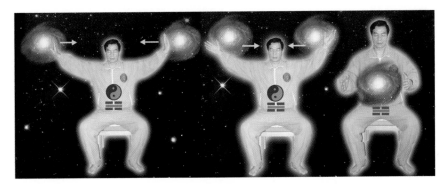

Fig. 5.7. Completing the kan trigram

6. **Repeat the kan:** Rest. In your mind, repeat the word *kan* at the lower abdomen and let your eyes look down at the lower abdomen. Then close your eyes and visualize the symbol for kan (yin yang

Fig. 5.8. Kan in the abdomen

yin). Smile and be aware of the power of the yin, the gathering power, and be aware of the kidneys and ears, and try to imagine them in your mind's eye. Feel them imprinted on your abdomen and vibrating inside you.

7. **Project the trigram:** Rest, and project the trigram into the universe (see fig. 5.8 on the previous page). Feel the kan symbol in the universe reinforce the kan in the abdomen.

🌀 Li: The Second Sound

Li is the second sound (yang yin yang) and the power symbol of fire, the prospering power, connected with the heart. The eyes look up at the upper abdomen, the place of the li kua. The sound comes out from the area between the chest and the throat. Repeat the li sound until you feel the vibration of the fire expanding upward in the chest. When you chant *li*, you feel the energy rising. When you say *li*, the eyes look up.

1. **Chant li:** Chant the name of the trigram li in a long and deep voice while you visualize the symbol and touch your lower abdomen and upper abdomen (fig. 5.9).

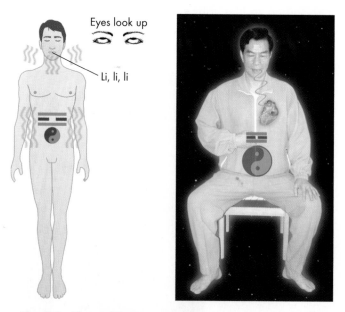

Fig. 5.9. Chant *li* (tongue and heart connect to the li).

2. **Chant the trigram:** Next, chant the yang and yin lines of the symbol one after the other *(yang yin yang)*. Start from the inner side close to the Tai Chi symbol.

3. **First line, yang expansion:** Be aware of the tan tien, throat, and crown, and the palms close to the navel, and slowly chant the long yang sound. Turn the palms out and gradually move the hands outward to the left and right. Feel your palms very long and big as they touch the cosmos. Rest in the expanded position and feel your palms touch the cosmic chi (fig. 5.10).

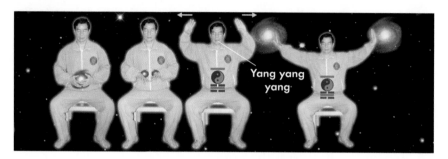

Fig. 5.10. Yang line: expand

4. **Middle line, yin contraction:** Your mind and the hands and palms touch the sky, the cosmos. Chant the *yin, yin, yin* as long as you feel comfortable, and continue moving your palms up. Draw in the cosmic chi from the universe into the navel, and feel that the navel has suction. Feel your hands and the tan tien. The throat has the power to draw the chi down into the yin line to the navel (fig. 5.11). Rest for a while.

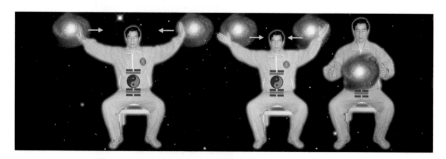

Fig. 5.11. Yin line: contract

5. **Last line, yang expansion:** Be aware of the tan tien, the throat, and the crown, and the palms close to the navel. Slowly chant the long yang sound. Turn the palms out and gradually move the hands outward to the left and right. Feel your palms very long and big as they touch the cosmos. Rest, feeling your palms touch the cosmic chi (fig. 5.12).

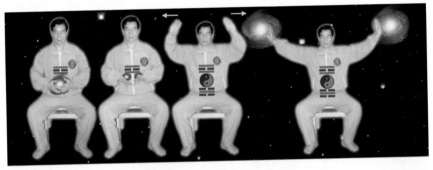

Fig. 5.12. Completing the li trigram

6. **Repeat the li:** Repeat the word *li* in your mind and let your eyes look at your li kua. Close your eyes and picture the li symbol, moving your eyes to look upward. Smile and be aware of the heart and the tongue, and the prospering power of fire. Imagine them in your mind's eye; feel them imprinted on your abdomen and vibrating inside you.

7. **Project the li:** Rest. Project the symbol into the universe. Feel the symbol in the universe reinforcing the li in the abdomen (fig. 5.13).

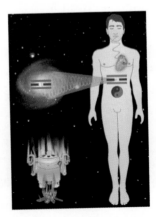

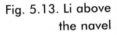

Fig. 5.13. Li above the navel

⊙ Chen: The Third Sound

Yin
Yin
Yang

Chen is the third sound (yang yin yin), the power symbol of thunder and lightning. Chen is connected with the liver and the eyes, the wood element and gathering power. This sound evokes the chen kua, the chen trigram whose place is on the right side (below the liver), and the sound is pronounced as "djen." Repeat the sound until you feel a vibration of energy below the liver, at the right side of the pakua. When you chant *chen*, the eyes look to the right side (fig. 5.14).

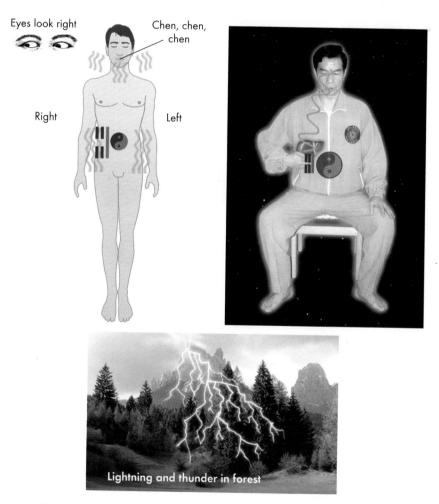

Eyes look right

Chen, chen, chen

Right

Left

Lightning and thunder in forest

Fig. 5.14. Chant *chen* (eyes and liver connect to the chen).

1. **Chant chen:** First chant the name of the trigram chen ("djen") in a long deep throat sound while picturing the symbol and touching the right side of your abdomen. Feel the vibration of the lightning and the thunder.

2. **Chant the trigram:** Look to the right side of the body, close your eyes, and visualize the symbol there, starting from the inside closest to the center. Chant the lines of the symbol (yang yin yin). Smile and be aware of the liver, the eyes, and the power of gathering, lightning and thunder power. Feel the vibrations inside as you chant the trigram.

3. **First line, yang expansion:** Be aware of the tan tien, throat, and crown and the palms close to the navel, and slowly chant the long yang sound. Turn the palms out and gradually move the palms to the left and right sides and feel your palms very long and big, touching the cosmos. Chant the *yang, yang, yang* as long as you feel comfortable. Rest for a while (fig. 5.15).

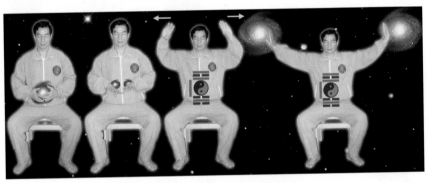

Fig. 5.15. Yang line: expand

4. **Middle line, yin contraction:** With your mind and your palms touching the cosmos, chant the yin sound as the palms touch the universe. Chant the *yin, yin, yin* as long as you feel comfortable and continue moving your palms back. Draw the cosmic chi from the universe into the navel and feel the navel has suction. Feel your hands and the tan tien; the throat has the power to suck the chi down to the yin line at the navel. Rest for a while (fig. 5.16).

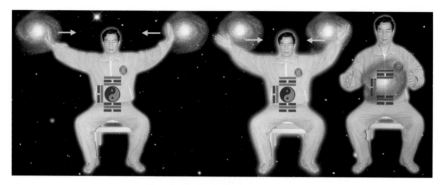

Fig. 5.16. Yin line: contract

5. **Last line, yin contraction:** Do the yin contraction as before; be aware of the tan tien, throat, and crown while the palms move out to touch the universe. Chant the *yin, yin, yin* as long as you feel comfortable, and continue moving your palms back to draw the cosmic chi from the universe into the navel. Feel the navel has suction. Feel your hands and the tan tien; the throat has the power to draw down the chi down to the yin line at the navel. Rest for a while (fig. 5.17).

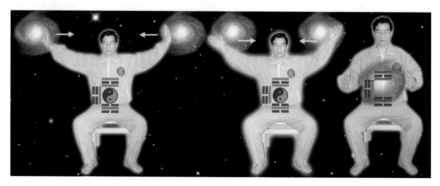

Fig. 5.17. Completing the chen trigram

6. **Repeat the chen:** Repeat the word *chen* ("djen") in your mind and let your eyes look to the right. Close your eyes and picture the chen kua, with your eyes looking right. Smile and be aware of the liver and the eyes, and the gathering power of wood. Rest for a while and feel the vibrations inside; feel the energy imprinted on your abdomen.

7. **Project the chen:** Project the symbol into the universe. Feel the symbol in the universe reinforcing the chen in the abdomen.

🌀 *Tui: The Fourth Sound*

Tui is the fourth sound (yang yang yin) and the power symbol of lake and rain, connected with the lungs and nose, the metal element, and contracting power. This sound evokes the tui kua that is placed on the left side (opposite chen), and the sound comes out as "tway." Chen and tui ("djen" and "tway") are throat sounds. You should repeat the sound until you feel a vibration of energy at the left side of the pakua (fig. 5.18).

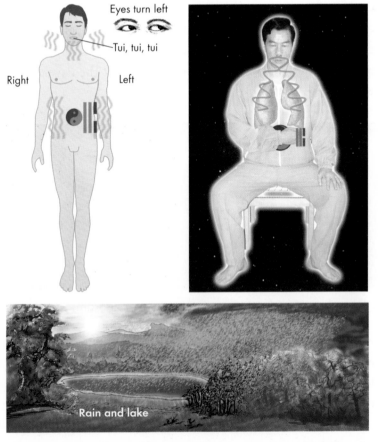

Fig. 5.18. Chant *tui* (nose and lung connect to the tui).

1. **Chant tui:** Chant the name of the trigram tui in a long deep voice while picturing the symbol and touching the left side of your abdomen. Feel the vibration of the rain and the lake.

2. **Chant the trigram:** Chant the lines of the tui kua one after the other *(yang yang yin)*, starting from the inside, closest to the Tai Chi symbol.

3. **First line, yang expansion:** Be aware of the tan tien, throat, and crown, and palms close to the navel, and slowly chant the long yang sound. Turn the palms out and gradually move the palms to the left and right sides, feeling your palms very long and big, touching the cosmos. Chant the *yang, yang, yang* (fig. 5.19).

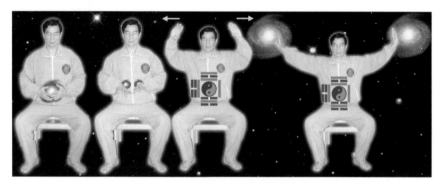

Fig. 5.19. Yang line: expand

4. **Middle line, yang expansion:** Be aware of tan tien, throat, and crown, palms close to the navel, and slowly chant the long yang sound. Turn the palms out and gradually move the palms to the left and right sides, and feel your palms very long and big, touching the cosmos. Chant the *yang, yang, yang.*

5. **Last line, yin contraction:** With your mind, hands, and palms touching the sky and the cosmos, chant the *yin, yin, yin* as long as you feel comfortable. Continue moving your palms to draw the cosmic chi from the universe into the navel, and feel the navel has suction. Feel your hands and the tan tien; the throat has the power to draw the chi down to the yin line at the navel. Rest for a while (see fig. 5.20 on the following page).

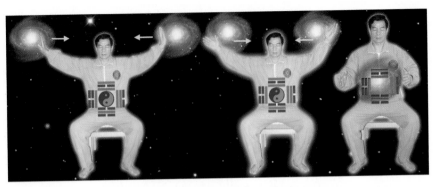

Fig. 5.20. Completing the tui trigram

6. **Repeat the tui:** Repeat the word *tui* ("tway") in your mind. With eyes closed and looking to the left, see your tui kua in its place on the left side (yang yang yin). Smile and be aware of your lungs and nose, and the contracting power of rain and lake, and of metal. Feel the trigram and its energy imprinted on your abdomen and vibrating inside you.

7. **Project the tui:** Rest. Project the tui symbol into the universe. Feel the symbol in the universe reinforcing the tui in the abdomen.

Combine the Four Trigrams

When you finish the imprinting of these first four symbols, you will make the Tai Chi symbol, spiraling with your fingers around the navel and chanting: *Tai Chi, Tai Chi, Tai Chi.* This is an abdominal sound. Continue to chant it inwardly, *Tai Chi, Tai Chi, Tai Chi,* at the same time spiraling with your fingers and, gently, with your eyes. When you finish the chanting, rest. Feel the kan, the li, the chen, and the tui join together, fusing the energy of these forces inside of you.

1. First look at your pakua and say the name of the symbols and their yin-yang components.

2. Chant *kan, li, chen, tui* while moving your eyes down, up, right, left. Repeat several times. Rest.

3. Spiral with your fingers around the navel and gently make a spiraling movement of the eyes while chanting *Tai Chi, Tai Chi, yin yang,*

yin yang until you feel the Tai Chi symbol spiraling in the middle of the pakua, connecting the trigrams together. Feel a big space, with a fire burning inside of you.

Creating the Front Pakua: The Next Four Symbols

The last four trigrams of the pakua are: kun (yin yin yin), the earth power; ken (yin yin yang), the mountain power; sun (yin yang yang), the wind power; and chien (yang yang yang), the heaven power.

 *Kun: The Fifth Sound*

Kun is the fifth sound (yin yin yin) and the power symbol of earth, the stabilizing power of harmony. It is connected with the stomach and mouth, spleen, and pancreas. The kun trigram is located on the upper left (northwest) side of the pakua.

1. **Chant and draw the kun:** Focus on kun (yin yin yin). Chant *kun* and then chant *yin, yin, yin* repeatedly, and mark the lines on your forehead with your fingers and your mind's eyes. You can use the hand to help draw in the energy back to the pakua. Later on, you do not need to use your fingers.

2. **Do the three lines:** Make the yin contraction for each line of the trigram.

3. **Expand the kun:** Picture the kun symbol in front of you and expand it very far away to connect with the centering, stabilizing power. Let the energy with the symbol come to you until it sticks to your forehead. Bring it down to the northwest (upper left) corner in the abdominal pakua (see fig. 5.21 on following page).

 *Ken: The Sixth Sound*

Ken is the sixth sound (yin yin yang) and the power symbol of mountain. It is a stable and strong energy, connected with the bladder, the right sexual organs, and the back of the skull.

Fig. 5.21. Chant *kun* (earth, mouth, and spleen connect to the kun).

1. **Chant and draw the ken:** Focus on ken (yin yin yang). Chant first *ken* and then *yin, yin, yang* repeatedly. It is a nose/throat sound. Mark the symbol with your fingers and your mind's eye on your forehead.

2. **Do the three lines:** Make the first yin contraction, the middle yin contraction, and the last yang expansion.

3. **Expand the ken:** Rest and feel the symbol imprinted on your forehead. Expand it far away to make the connection with the stable and strong mountain power. Feel the symbol with the energy come back. Move it to its place in the pakua on your abdomen in the lower right corner (fig. 5.22).

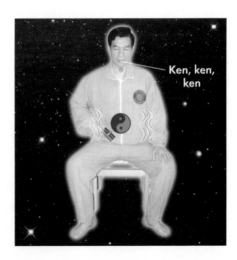

Fig. 5.22. Chant *ken* (mountain connects to the back of the skull).

🌀 *Sun: The Seventh Sound*

Sun is the seventh sound (yin yang yang) and the power symbol of wind. It is connected with the gallbladder and the base of the skull.

1. **Chant and draw the sun:** Focus on sun (yin yang yang). Chant *sun* and then *yin, yang, yang* repeatedly. Picture the symbol on your abdomen; mark it with your fingers at the abdomen first and then just with your eyes and mind.

2. **Do the three lines:** Make the first line's yin contraction, the middle line's yang expansion, and the last line's yang expansion.

3. **Expand the sun:** Picture the symbol very far away to connect with the power of the wind until it comes back to you and sticks to your abdomen. When the reinforced symbol sticks to your abdomen, move it down to its place in the upper right corner of your abdominal pakua (fig. 5.23).

Fig. 5.23. Chant *sun* (wind connects to the base of the skull).

🌀 *Chien: The Eighth Sound*

Chien is the eighth sound (yang yang yang) and the power symbol of heaven, the expanding yang energy. It connects with the left sexual organs, the large intestine, and the forehead bone.

1. **Chant and draw the chien:** Focus on chien, yang yang yang. Chant *chien* and then *yang, yang, yang* repeatedly. Mark the lines of the trigram on the abdomen with your fingers and your eyes/mind.

2. **Do the three lines:** Make the yang expansion for each of the three lines.

3. **Expand the chien:** Rest and feel the symbol imprinted on the abdomen. Expand it very far away to connect with the power of heaven. Do it several times until you feel that the symbol is coming back and sticks on your abdomen. Bring this reinforced trigram down to its place in the lower left corner of your abdominal pakua (fig. 5.24).

Fig. 5.24. Chant *chien* (heaven connects to the forehead bone)

Chien, chien, chien

✿ Combine the Eight Trigrams

Go through the same procedure as with the first four symbols to evoke the energy and connect it to the pakua, spiraling with your fingers around the navel.

1. Look at your pakua and say the name of each symbol and its yin and yang components.

2. Chant all the eight symbols together quickly: *kan, li, chen, tui, kun, ken, sun, chien.* Do 6 sets.

3. Be aware of the completed pakua and see it imprinted deep into the abdomen.

4. Be aware of the Tai Chi symbol and start to chant, *Tai Chi, Tai Chi, Tai Chi*, faster and faster. Feel the Tai Chi symbol spiraling faster and faster now (fig. 5.25).

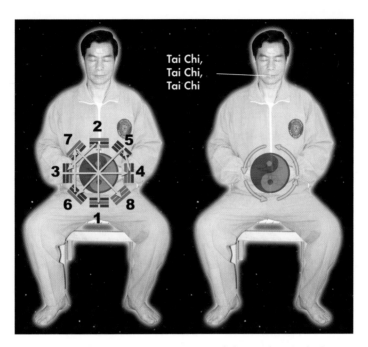

Fig. 5.25. Finish the imprinting of the eight symbols, the complete pakua.

Forming Four Pakuas and Establishing the Cauldron

Now that we have a fully formed front pakua with which to draw in the eight forces and connect with the organ energies, we can replicate the pakua image and use the pakuas to form the cauldron. The cauldron is considered the center of the body. It is located in the space between the navel and the Door of Life, slightly more toward the back of the body. The exact center can vary with each person. The cauldron is the place of universal force and the place where all of the forces combine and transform to a higher energy. Students first work with the cauldron in the Fusion of the Five Elements practice.

⊙ Create the Back Pakua, Merge the Energy, and Establish the Cauldron

1. Copy the front pakua to the back in order to create the back pakua. Let the Tai Chi symbol spiral. Be aware of the front pakua spiraling in one direction and the back pakua moving in the opposite direction (fig. 5.26). You can start the front pakua spiraling counterclockwise and the back clockwise. Be aware of the center of the tan tien, and form a space there for the cauldron. At this point, leave the spinning energy moving. Feel both pakuas still spinning and drawing cosmic force from all directions. Rest, and again be aware of the spiraling energy.

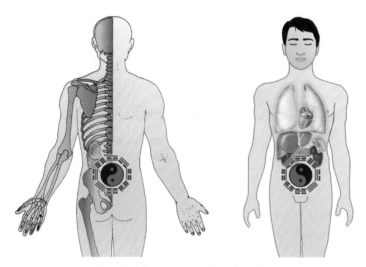

Fig. 5.26. Front and back pakuas

2. When both pakuas are spiraling, focus on the center, and look down while remaining aware of the front and the back pakuas (fig. 5.27). Chant *yin, yang* and spiral with your mind's eye in the center. Feel the space of the front pakua and the back pakua coming into the center, merging together and creating a big space inside you for the

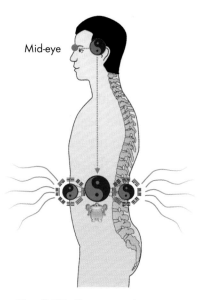

Mid-eye

Fig. 5.27. Focus on the center.

cauldron. Feel the cauldron inside you spiraling like a big ball of fire, creating a suction in the middle between the front and the back pakua. Feel that, while you continue to chant the Tai Chi subvocally, the energies of both pakuas are sucked into the center, the cauldron. Feel the fire burning in the cauldron like a candle. Be aware of your center and of the energy there (fig. 5.28).

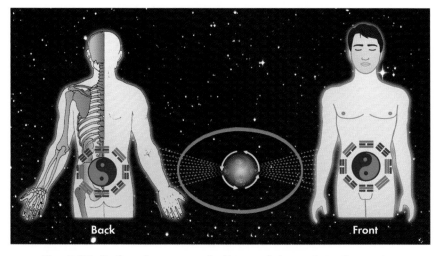

Back   Front

Fig. 5.28. Both pakuas are spiraling and drawn into the center.

🌀 *Create the Right Pakua*

The right pakua is a copy of the back pakua moved to the right side.

1. Use your finger to point to your right side on the same level with the navel while you visualize the pakua. Then, with your finger, draw the Tai Chi symbol, and begin to spiral it, from the bottom to the right to the top and to the left.
2. Chant the Tai Chi and follow the spiraling with your fingers at the same time. When you feel that you are in the rhythm, continue the motion using your mind's eye.
3. Rest. Feel the pakua spiraling and drawing energy.

🌀 *Create the Left Pakua*

This pakua is a copy of the front pakua moved to the left side.

1. Use your finger to point to your left side on the same level with the navel while you visualize the pakua. Draw the Tai Chi symbol, and begin to spiral it.
2. Chant the Tai Chi, and spiral with your hand in the middle of the left pakua. When you are ready, continue spiraling with your mind's eye until you feel the energy moving.
3. Rest. Feel the pakua spiraling and drawing energy.

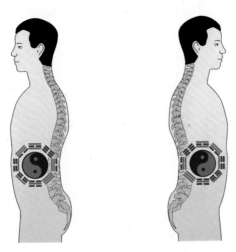

Fig. 5.29. Left and right pakuas

⊙ Merge the Energies of the Four Pakuas in the Cauldron

1. Bring your attention back to the right pakua, activate it, and let the Tai Chi spiral.
2. Bring your attention back to the left pakua and reactivate it, spiraling the Tai Chi.
3. Focus on your center as you chant the Tai Chi, and be aware of the centers of the front, back, right, and left pakuas. Feel that the energies of the pakuas are sucked into the center. Feel the energy become violet light; feel and see the center spiraling with your mind's eye (fig. 5.30).

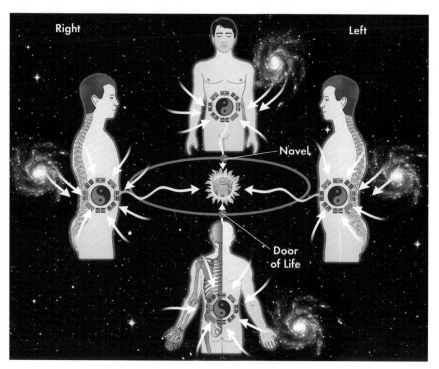

Fig. 5.30. Four pakuas spiral and are drawn into the center of the cauldron.

Connecting the Organs and Senses with
the Abdominal Pakua

1. Bring your ears' and kidneys' energy to the kan trigram on the
   bottom of the pakua (fig. 5.31).

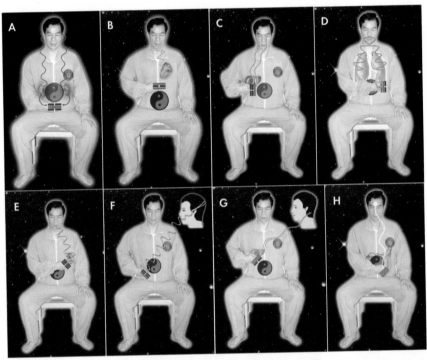

Fig. 5.31. Connecting the organs

A. Kan—Ear and kidneys; **B.** Li—Tongue and heart; **C.** Chen—Mid-eyebrow and liver;
D. Tui—Lung and nose on left side; **E.** Kun—Mouth and upper left side;
F. Ken—Back of the skull; **G.** Sun—Base of the skull; **H.** Chien—Forehead point

2. Bring the tongue and heart energy to the li trigram on the top.
3. Bring the mid-eyebrow and the liver energy to the chen trigram
   on your right side.
4. Bring the lungs and nose energy to the tui trigram on your left
   side.
5. Bring your mouth energy to the kun trigram on your upper left
   side.

6. Connect the back part of your skull to the ken trigram on your lower right side.

7. Connect the base of the skull to the sun trigram on your upper right side.

8. Connect the forehead point to the chien trigram on your lower left side.

Spiral the Tai Chi of this pakua, drawing all the energy of the organs and the senses to the center, where all these energies are combined and condensed.

THE PAKUAS OF THE HEAD

The forehead pakua is the reverse of the abdominal pakua. Use the fingers to point at the position of the pakua. Later on, mark the symbol with your eyes and mind. The yin and yang sounds generate from the abdomen but also with emphasis on the throat, nasal passages, and the third eye (fig. 5.32).

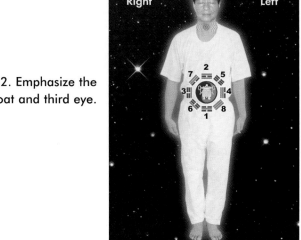

Fig. 5.32. Emphasize the throat and third eye.

When you rest after making the specific sound, feel that the symbol of the trigram is imprinted on the forehead. Send this symbol out into the space in front of you to make the connection with the force of the universe and then let it come back to your body. Bring this reinforced symbol down to the trigram in the pakua in the abdomen and start to work with the next symbol.

 ## Preparing to Form the Facial Pakua

To practice this stage, we form a pakua on the face. This pakua has its face in front of you (as if the symbol is looking toward you), so that the chen will be on the left side and the tui will be on the right side, and all the other trigrams will be arranged accordingly. The Tai Chi symbol centers on your mid-eyebrow and spans up to the forehead and down to the ridge of the nose right where the cavity of the spirit is. All the senses are controlled from this point. When information/energy from outside is coming in to trigger the senses, you will feel it first very strongly in this center, and then your senses will connect immediately to the center of the front pakua below (fig. 5.33).

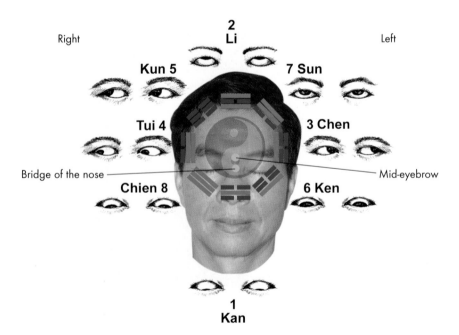

Fig. 5.33. Use the eye-mind power "I" to help move the eight forces.

1. In order to help you get more chi from the universe, you can start with the practice called Opening the Three Tan Tiens to the Six Directions (fig. 5.34), which is given in the book *Taoist Cosmic Healing* (Destiny Books, 2003). If you have not learned this practice, you can just start with forming the pakua.

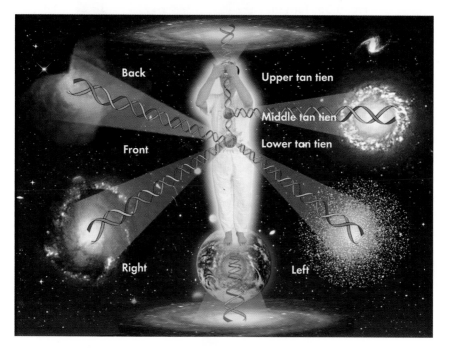

Fig. 5.34. Opening the three tan tiens to the six directions

2. Smile, feel your senses turned inward, feel them connecting to the organs (see fig. 5.35 on the following page). Your mid-eyebrow connects to your eye and liver, your tongue connects to the heart, your ears connect to the kidneys, your nose connects to your lungs, and your mouth connects to the spleen. Feel all the senses turned inward to the mid-eyebrow and down to the navel, going deep inside. Your abdomen is like a big ocean, a whole universe.

3. Be aware of the three fires and feel them burning: the kidney fire, the heart fire, and the tan tien fire. Feel your lower tan tien expanding and contracting with your breathing (see fig. 5.36 on the following page).

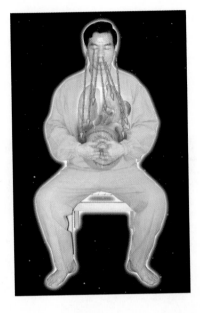

Fig. 5.35. Turn all senses inward.

4. Turn your attention to your heart center and feel the space of this heart center getting bigger and forming the pakua around the heart and radiating out the electromagnetic field. Recent research has revealed that the heart generates a strong electromagnetic

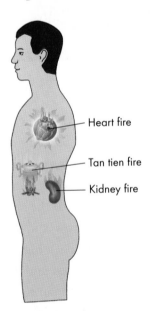

— Heart fire

— Tan tien fire

— Kidney fire

Fig. 5.36. Activate the three fires.

field within and around the body. The electrical field is shaped like a donut, or torus, similar to the biomagnetic field of the human aura, and the geomagnetic field of the Earth. Focus also on your upper tan tien (brain); feel the space there getting bigger as well. The electricity manifests as an electrical field within and around the body, subtle but detectable.

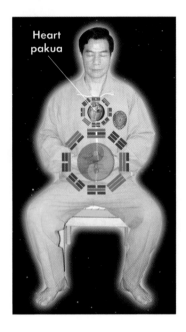

Fig. 5.37. Touch the lower tan tien and chant.

5. Reactivate and reinforce the pakua in your lower abdomen. Touch your lower tan tien and start chanting *kan, li, chen, tui, kun, ken, sun, chien,* touching each of the kuas as you chant it. Continue to chant the kua symbols subvocally in your mind while holding the symbol in front of your eyes. Be aware of the heart pakua (fig. 5.37).

6. Spiral the Tai Chi symbol from the bottom to the right and up, chanting it while spiraling with your hand, eyes, and mind. Continue to spiral with your mind and eyes only and feel the heart pakua also spiraling. The energy is pulling inward and the Tai Chi symbol is spiraling and changing to violet light (see fig. 5.38 on on the following page).

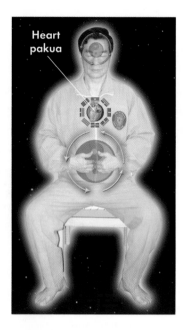

Heart
pakua

**Fig. 5.38. Tai Chi
symbol spiraling**

 Creating the Facial Pakua, Forming the
Eight Symbols

 Activate the Kan—Water

1. **Draw and chant the kan:** Be aware of the mid-eyebrow. Use the
   fingers of either the right or left hand to touch below your nose.
   Eyes look down to the bridge of the nose. Focus on the kan (yin
   yang yin). Chant the word *kan* repeatedly, vibrating it in the brain,
   making a throat, nose, and third eye sound (fig. 5.39). Chant the
   lines, *yin yang yin, yin yang yin.* Picture the trigram on your face
   and expand it very far away to the ocean. Feel that the energy of
   the kan comes right in front of you, allowing the feeling to expand
   on the bridge of the nose. Be aware of the kan in your lower abdomen and move the powerful kan from your face to its place in your
   lower abdomen.

2. **Yin contraction:** First expand the mind and the hands and palms
   to touch the sky, the cosmos (fig. 5.40). Chant the *yin, yin, yin* as
   long as you feel comfortable, and continue moving your palms.
   Draw the cosmic chi in from the universe into the face and feel

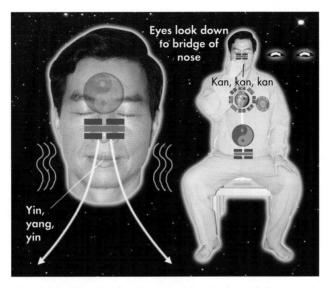

Fig. 5.39. Kan on the face (on the bridge of the nose)

Fig. 5.40. Yin line: contract

the mid-eyebrow has suction. Feel your palms, fingers, and the tan tien, the mid-eyebrow has power, the fingers can move in and touch below the nose. The chi goes to the yin line in the navel. Rest and smile, breathing the cosmic chi.

3. **Yang expansion:** Do the yang line; be aware of the tan tien, throat, bridge of the nose, the palms, and the fingers and touch the face. Slowly chant the long yang sound and turn the palms out. Gradually move the palms to the left and right sides and feel your

palms very long and big, touching the cosmos. Rest and smile; the chi goes to the yang line in the navel (fig. 5.41).

Note: Any time that you feel the energy shooting into your forehead, right where the senses' control is located, bring both the energy of the senses and the energy from the universe down to your abdomen.

4. **Yin contraction:** Yin contracts; expand the mind. Repeat as in the first yin line. Rest for a while. Feel the vibrations inside (fig. 5.42).

Fig. 5.41. Yang line: expand

Fig. 5.42. Completing the kan trigram

☯ Activate the Li—Fire

1. **Draw and chant the li:** Focus on the li (yang yin yang) trigram. Draw it several times using your fingers on your mid-eyebrow,

starting with the line closest to the center (fig. 5.43). Eyes look up to the forehead and visualize a flame burning. Chant *li, li, li* repeatedly. Then chant the *yang, yin, yang*. Picture the trigram right on your face and expand it very far away. See a fire burning, expanding warmth. Let the energy come back and stay on your forehead as a bright red light. Bring it down to the li in the pakua in your abdomen and feel a burning sensation in that area.

2. **Yang expansion:** Do as before.
3. **Yin contraction:** Do as before.
4. **Yang expansion:** Do as before.

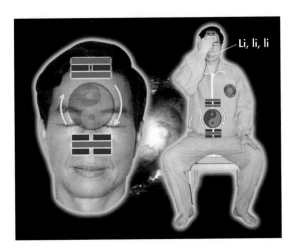

Eyes look up to forehead

Fig. 5.43. Li on forehead

Activate the Chen—Thunder

1. **Draw and chant the chen:** Focus on chen (yang yin yin). Chant the name of the symbol ("djen") as a throat and nose sound repeatedly, and then chant *yang, yin, yin*. The eyes look to the left temple bone (fig. 5.44). Picture the symbol in front of you, expand it very far away to the power of the lightning and thunder. Let the energy come to you; feel the tingling on your left temple bone and move this energy sensation down to the left side of the abdominal pakua. Be aware of kan, li, chen. Visualize them very clearly.

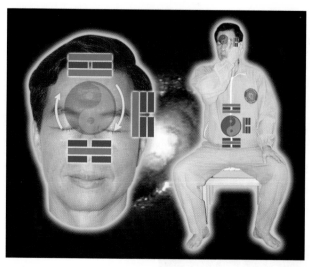

Eyes look to left temple bone

Fig. 5.44. Chen on left temple

2. Yang expansion: Do as before.

3. Yin contraction: Do as before.

4. Yin contraction: Do as before.

☯ Activate the Tui—Lake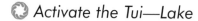

1. **Draw and chant the tui:** Focus on tui (yang yang yin). Chant *tui* ("tway") repeatedly with a nose sound that vibrates in the nose. Then chant *yang, yang, yin*; eyes look to the right temple bone (fig. 5.45). Picture the symbol on your right temple bone and expand it very far away to the power of the lake and rain, the metal element. It is a condensing power. Move it down to the right of the abdominal pakua.

2. **Yang expansion:** Do as before.

3. **Yin contraction:** Do as before.

4. **Yin contraction:** Do as before.

Combine the four symbols together with the Tai Chi symbol. Feel the Tai Chi symbol spiraling inside your head and feel the center of your abdomen nice and warm, as though a fire is burning inside you.

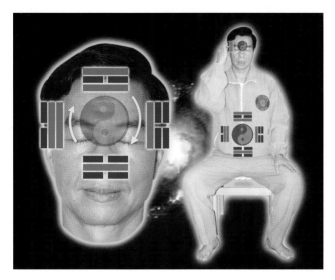

Eyes look to right temple bone

Fig. 5.45. Tui on right temple

Activate the Kun—Earth

1. **Draw and chant the kun:** Imprint kun (yin yin yin) on your forehead (see fig. 5.46 on the following page). Start chanting *kun, kun, kun,* and then *yin yin yin, yin yin yin.* Use the fingers and palms to help activate the cosmic force, marking the lines with your fingers on your forehead. Project the symbol into the universe as you breathe through your forehead. Picture the symbol breathing in violet/blue, and when you feel it connect to your forehead bring it down to its place in the lower pakua.
2. **Yin contraction:** Do as before.
3. **Yin contraction:** Do as before.
4. **Yin contraction:** Do as before.

Activate the Ken—Mountain

1. **Draw and chant the ken:** Imprint ken on your lower left cheek bone (see fig. 5.47 on the following page). Start with the eyes looking down to the lower left cheek bone; chant *ken, ken, ken,* and then *yin yin yang, yin yin yang,* marking the lines with your

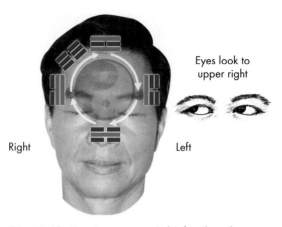

Eyes look to
upper right

Right   Left

Fig. 5.46. Kun on upper right forehead

fingers on your forehead. Project the symbol into the universe as
you breathe through your forehead. Picture the symbol with its
violet/blue and bright red colors in front of you, and when you
feel it connect to your forehead bring it down to its place in the
lower pakua.

2. Yin contraction: Do as before.

3. Yin contraction: Do as before.

4. Yang expansion: Do as before.

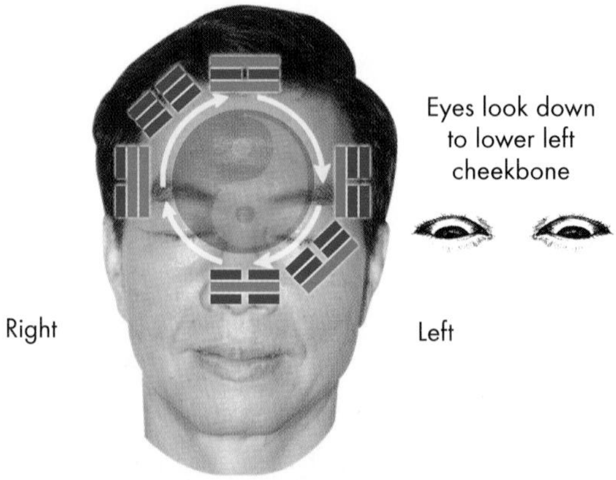

Eyes look down
to lower left
cheekbone

Right   Left

Fig. 5.47. Ken on left cheekbone

Activate the Sun—Wind

1. **Draw and chant the sun:** Imprint sun on your upper left eyebrow (fig. 5.48). Start with the eyes looking up to the upper left eyebrow; chant *sun, sun, sun,* and then *yin yang yang, yin yang yang, yin yang yang,* marking it with your fingers on your forehead. Project the symbol into the universe as you breathe through your forehead. Picture the symbol with its violet/blue and bright red colors in front of you, and when you feel it connect to your forehead bring it down to its place in the lower pakua.
2. **Yin contraction:** Do as before.
3. **Yin contraction:** Do as before.
4. **Yang expansion:** Do as before.

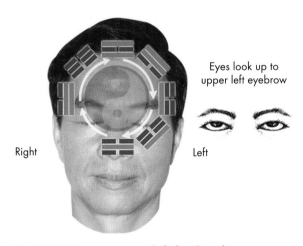

Eyes look up to upper left eyebrow

Right

Left

Fig. 5.48. Sun on upper left forehead

 Activate the Chien—Heaven

1. **Draw and chant the chien:** Imprint chien on your lower right cheek bone (see fig. 5.49 on the following page). Start with the eyes looking down to the lower right cheek bone, chanting *chien, chien, chien,* and then *yang yang yang, yang yang yang,* marking it with your fingers

on your forehead. Project the symbol into the universe as you breathe through your forehead. Picture the symbol with its bright red colors, and when it connects to your forehead, bring it down to its place in the pakua in your lower abdomen.

2. **Yang expansion:** Do as before.
3. **Yang expansion:** Do as before.
4. **Yang expansion:** Do as before.

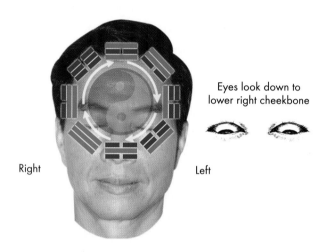

Eyes look down to lower right cheekbone

Right

Left

Fig. 5.49. Chien on right cheekbone

Note: Any time that you feel the energy shooting into your forehead, right where the senses' control is located, bring both the energy of the senses and the energy from the universe down to your abdomen.

�‍ Practicing with the Pakua on the Face to Turn the Senses Inward

1. Chant *kan, li, chen, tui, kun, ken, sun, chien* and mark the place of the specific kua with your fingers as follows for the facial pakua:

   - Kan is on the bridge of your nose.
   - Li is at the top of your forehead.
   - In the facial pakua, chen is on (inside) your left ear.

- Tui is on (inside) your right ear.
- Kun is in your brain above the right eye.
- Ken is inside your cheekbone on the left side.
- Sun is in your brain above the left eye.
- Chien is inside your cheekbone on the right side above.

2. Repeat the chanting in your mind and let your eyes move to the place of each kua. Feel the power of the symbols attracting your senses in to the mid-eyebrow.

3. Chant the Tai Chi symbol and spiral it, first with your finger and then only with your mind. Let the Tai Chi spin fast and faster. Keep on chanting the Tai Chi symbol until the energies are pulled to the center of the pakua. You should feel that all the energy is flowing to the center of the facial pakua and connecting to the center of the brain, the Crystal Room.

4. Keep on spiraling and be aware of the lower tan tien, the Tai Chi, and even the spiraling of the pakua itself. Feel a very strong center in your forehead and bring it down to the center of the lower pakua (fig. 5.50).

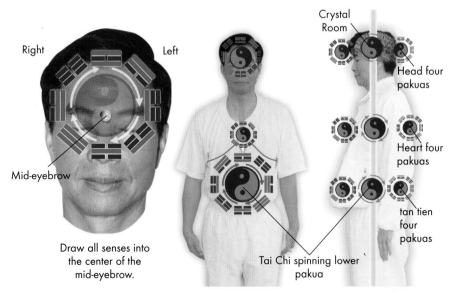

Fig. 5.50. Use the pakua on your face to turn the senses inward.

Creating the Four Pakuas on the Head

1. Duplicate the pakua with all the trigrams and the Tai Chi symbol
   to the back of the head, and spiral it clockwise while chanting the
   Tai Chi (fig. 5.51). The mind and the eyes are spiraling as well,
   going faster and faster. When you spiral as fast as possible, you will
   feel that the energy is drawing into the back pakua.

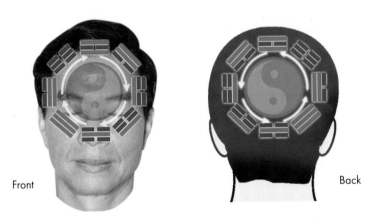

Front

Back

Fig. 5.51. Front and back pakuas on the head

2. Be aware of the front and back pakuas and spiral them. Spiral in
   the center faster and faster, drawing the front and back into the
   center (fig. 5.52).
3. Duplicate the front pakua to the left side of the head and let the
   Tai Chi symbol spin. Duplicate the back pakua to the right side of
   the head and let the Tai Chi symbol spin.

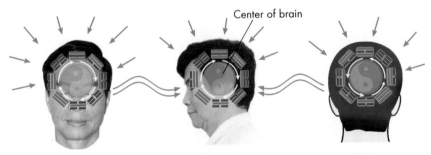

Center of brain

Fig. 5.52. Spiral faster and faster, drawing energy into the center.

4. Become aware of the center of the brain, the Crystal Room, and let it spin faster and faster, drawing the energy of the left and right pakuas into the center (fig. 5.53).

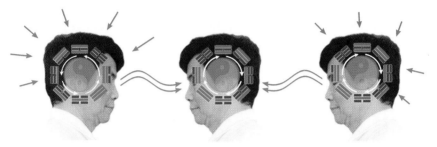

Fig. 5.53. Energy of the left and right pakuas moves into the center.

5. Be aware of the front, back, left, and right pakuas and let them spin. Bring attention to the center of the brain and let it spin faster and faster, drawing all the energy into the center (fig. 5.54).

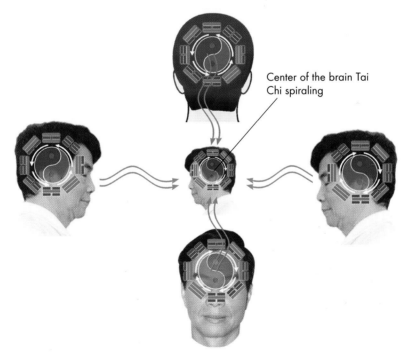

Center of the brain Tai Chi spiraling

Fig. 5.54. Draw all energy into the center.

Connecting the Senses with the Sense Control of the Facial, Heart, and Abdominal Pakuas

1. Repeat the facial pakua again: kan, li, chen, tui, kun, ken, sun, chien. This time, when you spiral the Tai Chi symbol as you chant Tai Chi, add the motion of the yin coming in and the yang going out. Your mouth is open, projecting the sound of yang into space. Your fingers are pointing out into space as well. With the sound of yin, your fingers are pointing in toward your forehead, which facilitates the inward movement of the energy.

2. Picture a Tai Chi spiraling inside your brain, right behind your forehead. Point, and spiral with your fingers, saying *yin yang, yin yang, yin yang,* and then *Tai Chi, Tai Chi, Tai Chi.* Continue saying it in your mind and feel the pakua deep inside your head (about 2 or 3 centimeters behind your forehead). All the senses are drawn together inside the center of the facial pakua (the senses' control point), and their energy is brought down to the Tai Chi of the lower abdominal pakua (fig. 5.55).

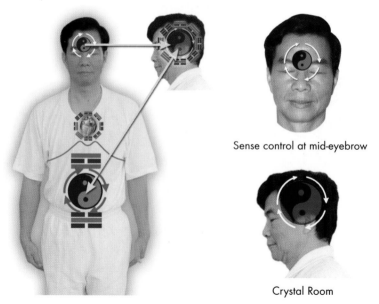

Sense control at mid-eyebrow

Crystal Room

Fig. 5.55. Let the center of the brain, the heart, and the abdomen pakuas and all Tai Chis spiral together.

Blending all the Energy of the Organs and Senses Together in the Cauldron

1. Look down to your center in the tan tien and focus on the pakua on the back and on the right and the left pakua. When you focus on them, they will just start spiraling on their own.
2. Look down into your center, into the cauldron, and start spiraling the Tai Chi symbol in the center of your cauldron while chanting *Tai Chi, Tai Chi, Tai Chi*. Rest.
3. Continue to spiral with only your mind, and feel that the energy of your senses and organs is coming right down to your center, where all the energy blends into one central energy.
4. Rest. Spiral the energy in your abdomen. Smile to this energy and feel very calm and peaceful (fig. 5.56).

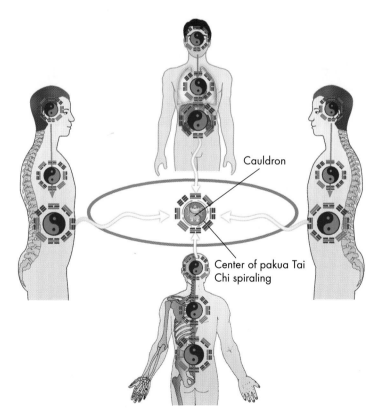

Cauldron

Center of pakua Tai Chi spiraling

Fig. 5.56. Draw all the senses into the center of the pakua and Tai Chi.

Expanding the Pakua in the Universe

The power of the symbol is the power of the throat, the power of the word. The forces of the universe are yin and yang forces, and the kua is a very ancient symbol of power. When you project the pakua out, using the pakua breathing, you connect to the yin and the yang power in the universe (fig. 5.57). When you breathe to the kua out there in space and connect to it, you will feel it connect to the kua in your abdomen as well (fig. 5.58).

Fig. 5.57. Feel the pakua breathing and pulsating.

Fig. 5.58. The pakua in the universe

1. Start chanting *kan, li, chen, tui, kun, ken, sun, chien,* touching each of the kuas on your abdomen as you chant them. Continue to do this with only your mind, saying the name of the kua and holding the symbol in front of your eyes. Then spiral the Tai Chi symbol from the bottom to the right and up, chanting it and spiraling with your hand, eyes, and mind. Continue to spiral with your mind and eyes only. Feel that the energy is drawn inward and the Tai Chi symbol is spiraling and changing to violet light.

2. Activate the facial pakua. Chant each of the symbols and point to them on your face; *kan, li, chen, tui, kun, ken, sun, chien.* Do this several times and then make the Tai Chi symbol on your forehead: Tai Chi, Tai Chi, Tai Chi, spiraling with your fingers over the third eye area. Feel the energy drawn into the center of the forehead, drawing the senses inward to the senses control and connecting down to the lower pakua. On their way down, they collect the energy from the organs as well.

3. Chant now *yin yang, yin yang, yin yang.* Contract with yin, and expand from the forehead out with yang. Use your fingers to point the direction of the energy, in and out.

4. Rest. Smile. Feel the Tai Chi very deep inside you spiraling, and chant *Tai Chi, Tai Chi, Tai Chi, Tai Chi.* Feel the facial pakua go into your head.

5. Become aware of the kan symbol. Picture the kan symbol and project it out and down, all the way to the galaxy. Chant *kan, kan, kan.* Chant and picture the yin yang yin lines, and feel that the power is going out all the way to outer space.

   Now start the yin-yang breathing: Inhale, yin contracting with bright violet light; exhale, yang expanding with bright red light. Inhale, contracting, exhale, expanding. Feel the kua of the facial pakua and the abdominal pakua breathing, and at the same time, feel the kua in the universe breathing. Picture the yin yang yin lines very clearly in your mind as well as very far away in space. Exhale, hold your breath and feel the symbol breathing. Inhale, breathe without breathing, and feel the connection with the kua out there. Keep on breathing in this way until suddenly the kan out there comes to you and enforces the kan in your abdomen.

6. Repeat the same procedure for li, sending it out and up into the universe; for chen, sending it out into the space on your right side; for tui, sending it to the space on your left side; for kun, sending it to the space in the upper left of the universe; for ken, sending it out and to the lower left side; for sun, sending it out and to the upper right side of the universe; and for chien, sending it out to the lower left side of the universe.

7. Now picture all the kuas together and repeat their names very slowly: *kan, li, chen, tui, kun, ken, sun, chien*. Rest. Feel the universal pakua covering you (fig. 5.59). Feel this pakua breathing and pulsating together with your pakua in the abdomen and on your face, drawing the energy back into the lower pakua, into your center. Sit back and smile to the pakua inside you and to the pakua in the universe. Rest, concentrate, and condense all the energies in the cauldron.

Fig. 5.59. Feel all the pakuas and universal pakuas breathing and pulsating. Feel a big pakua covering you, breathing and pulsating.

FORMULA TWO: TRANSFORMING THE NEGATIVE EMOTIONS OF EACH ORGAN INTO PURE LIFE FORCE ENERGY

Taoists reason that the negative emotions can be transformed to become our life force and positive energy. Therefore, to expel or suppress unwanted negative emotions is to expel or suppress life force. Rather than suppressing them, you gain more by composting and recycling—or experiencing these emotions and transferring the negative into positive energy. This means you permit them to emerge, observing and accepting them, but you do not let them run wild or trigger other negative emotions. Instead, you transform them not only into useful life force energy, but also into another, higher consciousness that is your spiritual energy (fig. 5.60).

Fig. 5.60. Transforming the negative emotions

A. Gather the emotions together, like piling all the garbage together.
B. Separate and transfer the emotions, like separating the garbage.
C. Recycle the food garbage into compost to grow flowers and vegetables.
D. Eat the food grown from the compost.

In the Taoist cosmology, the emotions originate from the vital organs, which correspond to the five phases of energy. They are also the reservoir of spiritual energy. By transforming the negative emotions in the organs, you nourish the spirit of that organ. Fear originates in and is stored in the kidneys; anger and frustration originate in and are stored in the liver; impatience, hastiness, and hatred originate in and are stored in the heart; sadness and depression originate in and are stored in the lungs; and worrying originates in and is stored in the spleen.

In the Tao, the main idea is to find a balance between the positive and the negative emotions. The negative emotions are very much like weeds: first, they are always there, and you can never totally get rid of them (fig. 5.61). Second, the soil (or the life force) needs them as fertilizers and to help hold the soil in place. But the danger is that they will take over the garden if we don't control them. We need to cultivate the plants we want (our good virtues) to prevent the weeds from taking over the garden. It is the same with the negative emotions; we should keep them in balance with the positive ones and not waste time trying to get rid of them altogether. We should work on the positive emotions, constantly cultivating and nurturing them in order to grow the good virtues and to keep the right balance with the negative

Fig. 5.61. Yin and yang balance negative and
positive emotions but they do not get rid of either.

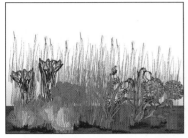

**Fig. 5.62. Keep on cultivating the positive emotions.
Do not let the weeds outgrow the vegetables.**

emotions. Negative emotions breed negative emotions, and positive emotions breed positive emotions (fig. 5.62).

We work in this formula with the counteracting or controlling cycle, and we use collection points to gather and neutralize the negative emotions of each organ. We then blend the emotional energies together in the pakua, transforming them into pure life force.

Transforming Negative Emotions

To begin, first do Formula 1 and then continue with this practice.

1. Sit properly on a chair and feel yourself aligned with the forces.
2. Do the crane and turtle neck and the Spinal Cord Breathing. (If you do not know these exercises, just begin with the Microcosmic Orbit.)
3. Do the Inner Smile meditation. Smile down and generate the qualities of loving energy from the heart. Breathe down radiance to the heart, making it feel soft (see fig. 5.63 on the following page).

Fig. 5.63. Feel joy and happiness.

A. Inhale to the heart and smile to the heart.
B. Exhale to the heart, smile to the heart, and make the heart feel soft.

4. Be aware of the tan tien chi and the front pakua, the pakua on your face, and the universal pakua. Feel them all breathing together. Feel all your senses and mind turned inward to the cauldron. Turning the senses inward initiates the training process of inner observation. In developing the ability to focus inward—to smell, taste, see, and hear the organs and their activities—and to observe your negative emotions without predetermined judgments, you have the opportunity to develop your true nature.

☯ Bring Your Attention to Your Kidneys

1. **Observe:** Listen to the kidneys; observe your kidneys. Be aware of any fear in the kidneys. Accept your fear; smile to the heart and let the love radiate to the kidneys.
2. **Activate the kan:** Be aware of the kan, the water power. Chant the kan and connect your kidneys with this energy. Let love activate the gentleness, calmness, and stillness, the essence of this power, a blue light. Wrap the gentle calmness around your fear, balancing it and transforming your fear.

3. **Collect and balance:** Form with your mind a collection point at your perineum and let any fear that is still in the kidneys go down to the collection point. Balance these emotions here also with the positive feeling of gentleness and calmness (fig. 5.64).

Fig. 5.64. Fear into gentleness and calmness

🌀 Bring Your Attention to Your Heart

1. **Observe:** Connect the tongue with the heart; speak with the spirit of your heart. Observe your heart. Be aware of any impatience, hastiness, cruelty, hatred, and arrogance in your heart. Accept these feelings.
2. **Activate the li:** Be aware of the li, the fire power. Chant the li and connect your heart with this power, a red light. Feel the warmth, love, happiness, and inner joy, the essence of this power. Help transform the hatred into love. Wrap the love, the warmth, and inner joy around your impatience and arrogance, balancing them

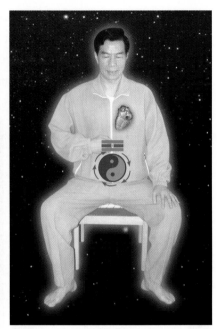

Fig. 5.65. Impatience, hastiness, and hatred into love, joy, and happiness

with and transforming your impatience, hastiness, and arrogance.

3. **Collect and balance:** Form with your mind a collection point near the heart center and spiral all the negative energies that are still in the heart to this collection point. Chant the li again and balance the emotions in the collection point (fig. 5.65).

Spiral, Blend, and Transform the Energy of the Heart and the Kidneys at the Front Pakua

1. Spiral and breathe the energies out of the kidney and heart collection points to the front pakua. Blend and spiral them together there. The pure energy trapped in the negative feelings will be freed and released to the center of the pakua (fig. 5.66).

2. Chant *Tai Chi, Tai Chi, Tai Chi, yin yang, yin yang, yin yang*. Spiral these energies until they become a bright, golden energy. This energy radiates love and gentleness from the center of the pakua and your being.

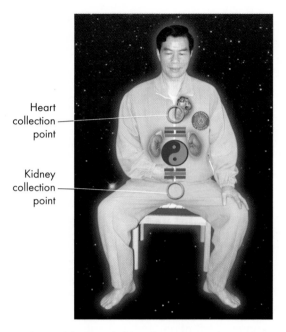

Heart
collection
point

Kidney
collection
point

Fig. 5.66. Spiral, blend, and transform the energy of
the heart and the kidneys.

Bring Your Attention to Your Liver

1. **Observe:** Connect the eyes with the liver and observe your liver. Be aware of any anger, frustration, aggressiveness, and guilt in the liver. Accept these feelings.
2. **Activate the chen:** Be aware of the chen. Chant the chen and connect your liver with the power of the thunder and the wood, a green light. Feel the kindness, the essence of the wood power. Wrap this feeling of kindness around your anger, balancing them together and transforming your anger. Feel that you can forgive. Forgiveness is one of the most important practices of the Taoist system.
3. **Collect and balance:** Form with your mind a collection point on the left side of the pakua, on the nipple line, and spiral all the negative energies that remain in the liver to this collection point. Chant the chen again, connect with the wood power and balance the emotions in the collection point (see fig. 5.67 on the following page).

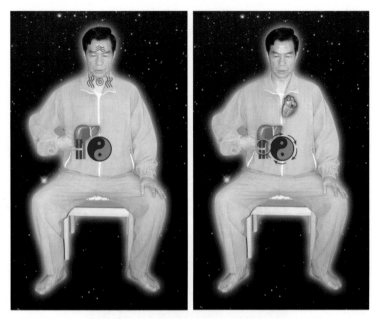

Fig. 5.67. Anger, frustration, and guilt into kindness

🌀 *Bring Your Attention to Your Lungs*

1. **Observe:** Connect the nose with the lungs and observe your lungs. Be aware of any sadness and depression in the lungs. Accept these feelings.

2. **Activate the tui:** Be aware of the tui. Chant the tui and connect your lungs with the power of the rain and the metal power, a white light. Feel the courage and the righteousness, the essence of the metal power. Wrap this courage around your sadness, balancing it with and transforming your sadness.

3. **Collect and balance:** Form with your mind a collection point on the right side of the pakua on the nipple line, and spiral any negative emotions that are still in the lungs to this collection point. Chant the tui again, connect with the metal power, and balance the sadness with the courage here again.

⊙ *Spiral, Blend, and Transform the Energy of the Liver and the Lungs at the Front Pakua*

1. Spiral and breathe the emotional energies from the liver and lungs collection points to the front pakua. Spiral and blend them at the front pakua. Feel that the pure energy that is trapped in the negative feelings will be freed and released to the center of the pakua (fig. 5.68).

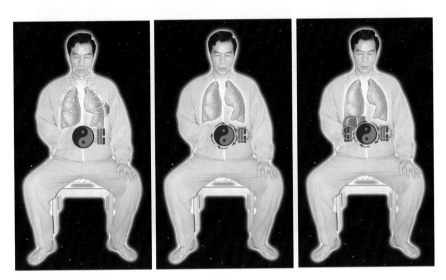

Fig. 5.68. Spiral, blend, and transform the energy of the liver and the lungs.

2. Chant *Tai Chi, Tai Chi, Tai Chi, yin yang, yin yang, yin yang*. Use the power of the pakua to balance and neutralize the sadness and anger. Continue to spiral the energies of the liver and lungs until they become a bright, golden energy that radiates kindness and courage from the center of the pakua and of your being.

⊙ *Bring Your Attention to Your Spleen*

1. **Observe:** Connect the mouth with the spleen and observe your spleen. Be aware of any worry or other emotions you do not like in your spleen.

2. **Activate the kun:** Be aware of the kun. Chant the kun and connect your spleen with the earth power, a yellow light. Feel the
openness, balance, and centeredness of this power, the essence of
the earth power. Wrap this around your worries, balancing with
and transforming your worries (fig. 5.69).

Fig. 5.69. Worry into balance, openness, and fairness

3. **Collect and balance:** Spiral any worries that are still in the spleen
to the center of the front pakua, the collection point of the spleen.
Chant the kun again. Then chant *Tai Chi, Tai Chi, Tai Chi, yin yang,
yin yang, yin yang.* Spiral, balance, blend, and transform the energy
with the energy that is already there into a bright, golden energy.

◌ Spiral All Remaining Negative Energy to the Front Pakua

Return your attention to the organs and the collection points, and
spiral and breathe to draw out any remaining negative energy. Blend
and neutralize it with the energy in the front pakua. See all the organs
glowing with light.

⊙ *Be Aware of the Back, Left, and Right Pakuas*

1. When you have time, you can chant the kuas to enforce the power of the pakuas. Let the Tai Chi in all four pakuas spiral, drawing in, blending, and transforming the energies.

2. Continue spiraling, and with the spiraling and the breath you draw, suck in the energy to the cauldron, the big empty space in the tan tien. Now spiral the energy in the cauldron, chanting the Tai Chi and the yin yang subvocally, condensing the energy into a bright golden energy ball, a pearl. Bring the pearl to the perineum and circulate it in the Microcosmic Orbit.

3. As the pearl moves through the Microcosmic Orbit, feel that it attracts and absorbs the universal force (at the crown), the cosmic particle force (at the mid-eye) and the earth force (at the perineum).

4. Bring the pearl back into the cauldron. Center yourself in the cauldron and feel your senses and mind drawn inward toward the energy in the cauldron. Feel nice, calm, and peaceful inside. When you have time, sit for a while and let this energy and feeling grow inside you (fig. 5.70).

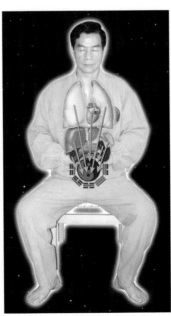

Fig. 5.70. Let all the organ energy flow down to the pakua and feel the chi grow inside you.

6

Compassion Fire Meditation and the Creation Cycle

The higher practice of Internal Alchemy is the transformation of the heart energy into love, the liver energy into kindness and generosity, the lung energy into courage, the kidney energy into gentleness, and the spleen energy into openness and fairness. We combine all these energies into compassion. Compassion becomes nonphysical energy that we can carry with us when we leave the world. It is the love and joy we feel within.

Fig. 6.1. Compassion fire originates from the heart.

Fig. 6.2. Through compassion fire, we transmit positive energy to our surroundings.

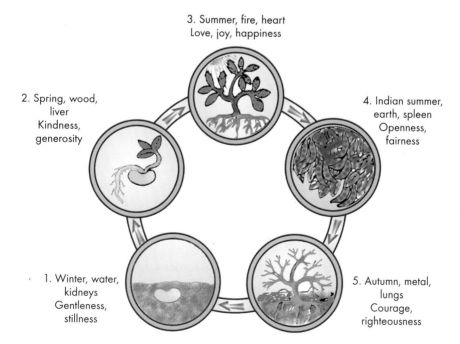

Fig. 6.3. The Creation Cycle in nature

We practice compassion through the act of forgiveness. To forgive is to let go. Always meet conflict with compassion.

Creating compassion energy begins with the Creation Cycle (see fig. 6.3 on the previous page). We activate the heart first, which is the place of the fire and the place where the virtue energies can be combined into compassion energy. We then go to the kidneys and bring their energy to the collection sphere. We continue with the liver, the heart again, the spleen, and the lungs, bringing the energy to the respective collection points (fig. 6.4).

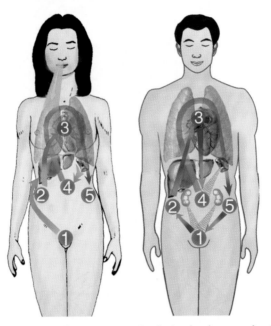

Fig. 6.4. The Creation Cycle in the human body

In the human body, the arousal state creates a new chemistry and a new vibration. This special vibration is measured at a frequency of 8 Hz/sec. According to both ancient and modern natural law, "As above, so below." In other words, as it is in the macrocosm, so it is in the microcosm. Hence, when you make love, all your cells and your DNA actually make love as well. The strands of the DNA cross over, like two serpents intertwining in an erotic embrace (fig. 6.5). They make love and they give birth. Any of the cells that do not reproduce will eventually die.

Fig. 6.5. When we feel love and arousal energy, the DNA
crosses over and makes love.

The two vital states are arousal, leading to orgasm, and compassion. Both are inextricably linked to love. When this love-vibration reaches the pineal gland, it produces a new hormone that creates whole-body conductivity. If the vibration is above or below the 8 Hz/sec. frequency, this process does not occur. It activates only when you feel the waves of orgasmic vibration and unconditional love for the self and others (figs. 6.6–6.8).

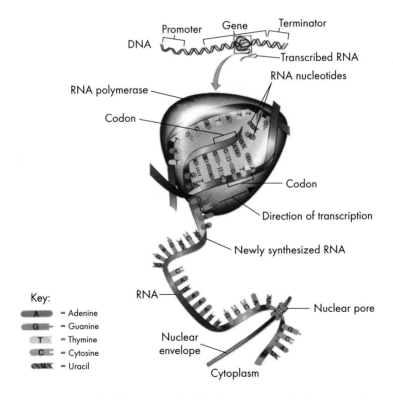

Fig. 6.6. When the frequency is 8 Hz/sec., transcription occurs in our cells' nuclei. During transcription, the genetic information in DNA is copied to RNA, which in the Tao is known as cupping or self-intercourse.

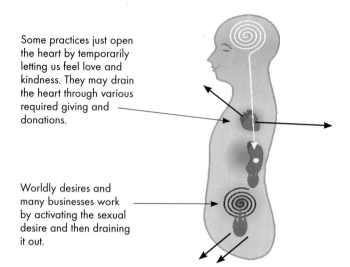

Some practices just open the heart by temporarily letting us feel love and kindness. They may drain the heart through various required giving and donations.

Worldly desires and many businesses work by activating the sexual desire and then draining it out.

Fig. 6.7. When the heart is only temporarily open and sexual desires activate, these forces will drain us out.

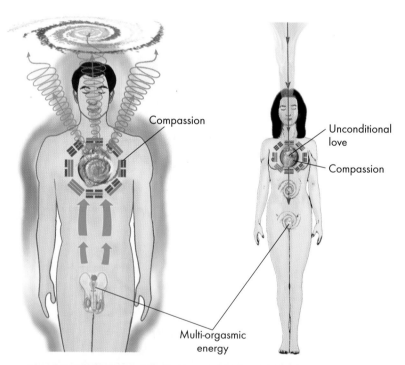

Compassion

Unconditional love

Compassion

Multi-orgasmic energy

Fig. 6.8. Through cultivating compassion energy, we can eventually build the one lasting energy.

Table 2. The Combination of Compassion Energy and Orgasmic Energy Is Lasting Energy

Heart energy	1. Heart energy is nonmaterial. When activated, it becomes love; but love does not last long.
	2. When all the good virtue energies from all the organs combine into one energy, it becomes compassion energy; it will last longer, but will still disperse.
Sexual energy	1. Sexual energy, when activated from material into nonmaterial, is powerful; but it will not last.
	2. When the sexual energy is aroused and changes into orgasmic energy, it can charge all the organs, glands, and senses, and it combines into one energy; this energy will last longer but will still disperse.
Combined energy	1. After the orgasmic energy has charged all the organs and created the multi-orgasm energy, it can then combine with the compassion energy at the tan tien. This creates the one energy that lasts the longest.
	2. When we are aware of the cosmic galaxy and expand our combined energy of compassion and orgasm through the universe, it multiplies and flows back to us, and connects us with universal compassion and unconditional love.

Creating the Compassion Fire

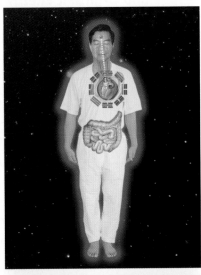

Fig. 6.9. Smile until you feel the heart soft with love, joy, and happiness.

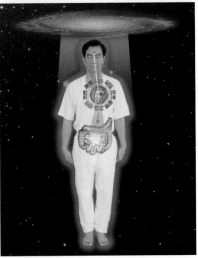

Fig. 6.10. Smile to the heart and the small intestine to make the heart feel soft. Feel the heart pakua spiral.

We can connect with the universal love.

1. Be aware of the tan tien and the universe, and feel the unconditional love flow down. Smile to the heart and small intestine (fig. 6.9, 6.10).

2. Smile to the spleen and let the love, joy, and happiness from the heart activate the energy of openness and fairness, the spleen's virtue energies (fig. 6.11).

Fig. 6.11. Let positive heart energies activate positive spleen energies.

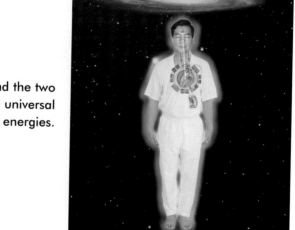

Fig. 6.12. Blend the two energies with universal energies.

3. Let the virtue energies flow back to the heart pakua and feel it spiral and blend together. Feel the yellow light flow from above and flow down to the heart (fig. 6.12).

4. Smile to the lungs and the large intestine. Send love from the heart to the lungs to activate their virtue energy of courage and righteousness (see fig. 6.13 on the following page).

5. Let the energy flow to the heart; feel it spiral and blend with

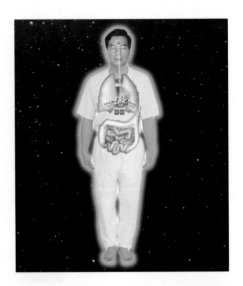

Fig. 6.13. Let love and joy from the heart activate positive lung energies.

Fig. 6.14. Blend the three energies into one energy.

love, joy, happiness, openness, and courage. Blend the three energies into one energy, and feel the white light from above flow into the lungs and the heart (fig. 6.14).

6. Smile to the kidneys and let the love of the heart activate the gentleness, softness, and calm in the kidneys (fig. 6.15).

7. Let the gentleness, softness, and calm in the kidneys flow into the heart. Blend and spiral the energies into one energy (fig. 6.16).

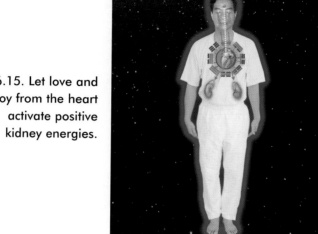

Fig. 6.15. Let love and joy from the heart activate positive kidney energies.

Fig. 6.16 Blend positive kidney energies with the compassion energy in the heart.

8. Smile to the liver and gallbladder. Let the softness and the love from the heart flow down to activate the kindness and generosity of the liver (see fig. 6.17 on the following page).

9. Let the kindness and generosity flow to the heart; feel it spiral and blend in the heart to become compassion; be aware of the green light flowing from above (see fig. 6.18 on the following page).

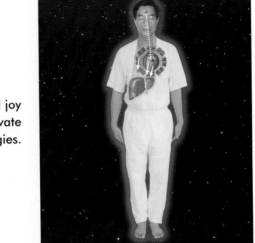

Fig. 6.17. Let love and joy from the heart activate positive liver energies.

Fig. 6.18. Blend positive liver energies into the compassion energy.

10. Smile to the heart and feel all the good virtuous energy from all the organs flow into the heart and spiral and blend into compassionate energy (fig. 6.19).

11. Your compassion rises up. Be aware of the galaxy and of the cosmos, and expand your compassion through the universe. The universe allows us to be in touch with the universal compassion (fig. 6.20).

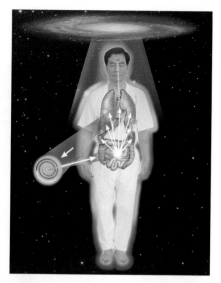

Fig. 6.19. All the organs' positive energies blend with the heart to create the compassion energy.

Fig. 6.20. Expand compassion to be in touch with the universal compassion.

Fig. 6.21. Let the universal compassion within us overflow.

12. Let the energy blend and multiply, and feel it flow back to enhance you. Feel your whole body to be filled with the universal compassion. You have such abundance, it overflows (fig. 6.21).

Sending Multi-Orgasmic Energy to the Sexual Organs

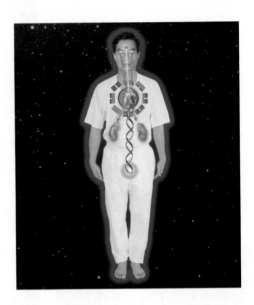

Fig. 6.22. Smile down to the heart, and feel warm heart energy flow down to the kidneys and the sexual organs.

1. Be aware of the sexual organs and use your hand to cover the sexual center. Smile, and feel the fire from the tan tien flow down (fig. 6.22).
2. Recall the times when you were with your loved one and had the high orgasmic feeling. Guide the orgasmic energy up to the kidneys, and feel the kidneys charge with chi and orgasm.
3. Guide the orgasmic energy spiraling up to the small and large intestines, liver, spleen, pancreas, stomach, and up to the lungs and heart. Continue up to the thymus, thyroid, and parathyroid, and up to the brain and the senses. Charge them all with orgasmic energy. Let the chi flow back down to the sexual organs and blend and spiral into one multi-orgasmic energy (fig. 6.23).
4. Be aware of the multi-orgasmic energy in the organs and bring it up to the crown, and let it continue to spiral up into the universe. Let the orgasm multiply. Be aware of the cosmic orgasm, and let it flow down to the crown. Feel all the cells fill with cosmic orgasm as it flows into the heart and then down to the sexual organs, filling them with compassion and cosmic orgasmic energy.

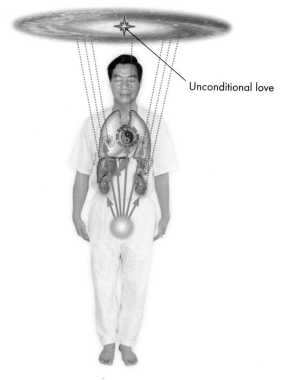

Unconditional love

Fig. 6.23. Bring the orgasmic energy spiraling up to the organs.

UNIVERSAL COMPASSION

Through the compassion practices, you will find your compassion rising up. Be aware of the multi-orgasmic sexual energy, and feel it combine with the compassion into one energy at the tan tien. Be aware of the galaxy and the cosmos, and expand your compassion throughout the universe. The universe puts you in touch with the universal compassion (see fig. 6.8 on page 110).

The compassion practice is the major practice for all the Fusion and Kan and Li practices. The compassion fire is the most important energy of the transformation. We will use it in all the practices.

Practice compassion through the act of forgiveness. To forgive is to let go. Always meet conflict with compassion (see figs. 6.24–6.28 on the following page).

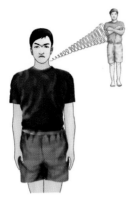

Fig. 6.24. Be aware of the people toward whom you feel resentment.

Fig. 6.25. People who make you feel angry

Fig. 6.26. People that you hate or people who hate you

Fig. 6.27. People who hurt you or people who have been hurt by you

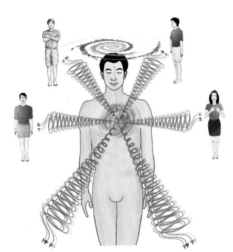

Fig. 6.28. Send out the abundance of compassionate energy that you have from the universe, to fill the person and to forgive whatever he/she did to you.

FUSING INNER POSITIVE ENERGY
WITH UNIVERSAL ENERGY

In Fusion I, we used the collection points to gather and store the energy of the organs. From the collection points in the body, we drew the energy down into the pearl. In Fusion II, we expand the collection points to encompass the energy body and the universal aura body. So, not only are we fusing the emotional energy of the physical body (emotions, senses, and thoughts), but now we also fuse the energy of the energy body and the universal body. This creates a much more complete practice and a highly refined pearl of energy. Fusing the elements is the secret to Internal Alchemy.

You can think of the different collection points as being like ingredients for a delicious soup. The more energy we can collect, the more spices we have for our soup. Alchemy is like cooking. What creates a really good dish is careful preparation of a combination of ingredients. Alchemy is about fusing the elements at our disposal to create balance and harmony within ourselves and the world we live in.

Learning a new recipe always takes some time and study, but once you have it in your mind, it is easy. The same is true with the Fusion practice. In the beginning of the Fusion practice, it all seems intricate and detailed. Once you get used to the formulas, it is a very easy and simple practice.

Fusion of the Five Elements introduced the collection points as a way to collect the negative energy from the organs. This energy was then directed into the pearl through the pakuas. Fusion I associated the collection points with the energy of the virgin children and the protective animals. In Fusion II, we are going to expand this practice by forming the collection points of the energy body and the collection points of the universal aura body. These collection points are a reflection of the collection points in the physical body.

The physical heart collection point is located at the heart center just behind the sternum. The energy body collection point is located at the lower tan tien at the top of the navel. And the universal aura body collection point is located above the head in the universe (fig. 6.29).

We utilize these collection points to create a powerful method of fusing all the elements into the pearl. Once we have established all the collection points, we rotate the collection points for the energy body and the universal aura body. This way, we have different colors at the various collection point sites. For example, the collection points at the energy body are turned clockwise—so that the green is on the upper point, red is at the left, white is at the bottom, and blue is on the right. The universal collection point is rotated counterclockwise—so that white is the upper point, blue is at the left, green at the bottom, and red at the right. Creating different colors at each of the collection points takes the fusing process to another level of intensity. We then mix these colors and blend them into the cauldron, and form them into a powerful pearl.

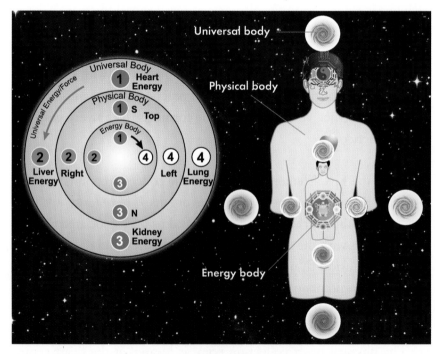

Fig. 6.29. Fuse inner positive energy with universal energy.

Fusing Inner Positive Energy with Universal Energy

We will use the four collection points of the elements fire, water, metal, and wood, in the middle of the physical body, in the energy body, and in the universal body. Once all the collection points are established in these three bodies, we use a dial to assist in rotating the patterns of energy.

You should understand the following:

- The physical body is relatively dense and stable; the collection points are fixed.
- The energy body is not fixed and is very sensitive to external events and the universe. This body can easily change.
- Universal energy is always changing and is not fixed. The planets' and the body's electrons, protons, nuclei, and cellular matter all move at different speeds. We use the differences to create energy.
- We use a dial of color to understand the different patterns of energy that can be created. Fusing different energies will generate more intense energy and a powerful pearl. Moving the color dials assists the imaginative mind to connect to the patterns of energy. It gives a formula, a pattern for the mind to follow.

In this approach, you fuse inside to outside universe and outside to inside universe. You mix fire and water first, then wood and metal. You can do it in pairs of points and then all four points, creating four balls of fused energy that are then spun very fast above the cauldron where they fuse to form a pearl. You can reproduce as many pearls as you want. The intensity can make you feel a oneness with the universe, as part of you does become part of the universe and the universal forces.

⟳ Forming the Pakuas and Collection Points

1. To begin, activate the three fires: The abdominal, the kidney, and the heart fires.

    Bring the fingertips to the navel. Feel the abdominal fire warming and opening the lower tan tien. The abdominal fire elicits deep awareness within the body. This awareness has the power to expand and connect to the entire universe.

    Bring the palms to the kidneys, the fingertips to the Door of Life. Feel the warmth in the kidneys, like a fire under the sea.

    Bring the hands to the heart, palms facing the chest. Visualize a glowing ball of light in the heart. Feel the warm radiant energy of compassion shimmering through the chest. Make the heart soft. Remember the yin within the yang.

2. Create the front pakua just behind the navel. Control the formation of the front pakua with assistance from the eyes, ears, nose, and mouth. As you balance the energy, let the pakua glow with light.

3. Chant the eight forces by sounding all the trigrams. Visualize the trigrams forming the front pakua. Chant the proper yin and yang combinations with each trigram.

4. Form the back pakua. Let it reflect off the front pakua like a mirror. In a similar manner, form the left and right side pakuas. Feel the energy starting to spiral and blend into the center of the abdomen.

5. Form the facial pakua. The facial pakua is the reverse direction of the abdominal pakua because we are looking at the pakua in front of the face. Feel the energy of the senses and the face gathered and collected. If you have time, chant the eight trigrams of the facial pakua.

6. Form the universal pakua. Feel the immensity of this pakua surrounding your entire body in every direction. Again, if time permits, chant the eight directions forming the pakua.

7. Be aware of the heart and all the good virtue energy, and fuse them together into compassion fire in the heart.

8. Be aware of the orgasm energy and multiply it to the organs, and

finally combine these energies into the heart, to become one compassion fire of unconditional love.

9. Form the collection points in the physical body. Feel the red light in the heart collection point, the blue light in the kidney collection point, the green light in the liver collection point, the white light in the lungs collection point, and the yellow light in the spleen collection point.

10. Remove negative energies from the organs. Use the senses to help locate the negative energies in the organs. Look deep inside; listen deep inside; smell deep inside; taste deep inside. Locate anything you find that you do not like. Spiral the negative energies into the collection points. Spiral them into the front pakua where they will blend and transform.

As you spiral the energies from all four pakuas into the cauldron, you are concentrating them in the cauldron of the body. The cauldron, as the center point of the human being, is the place that contains the essence of all sense, organ, and gland energies. The energy directed to the cauldron is transformed and stored for later use in the development of the soul and spirit bodies.

❁ Turning the Dial Once

Feel the reflection of the colors in the collection points in the energy body that surrounds the cauldron.

Feel the outward reflection of the collection points in the universe: the red ball of light above the head, the blue ball of light deep below the feet, the green ball of light to the right, and the white ball of light to the left.

1. Turn the collection points of the energy body clockwise one station. Turn the collection points of the universal body counterclockwise one station. The physical body collection points always remain stationary.

Now the color sequence at the top is red at the physical heart collection point, green below it in the energy body, and white above in the universal collection point. At the bottom, the physical collection point is blue, the energy body is white, the universal is green. At the right, the physical body collection point is green, the energy body is blue, and the universal is red. And on the left, the physical body is white, the energy body is red, and the universal is blue (fig. 6.30).

2. Now begin the fusion. Move down to fuse the white energy from the energy body with the blue ball in the physical collection point at the perineum, and fuse both of these energies down to the universal collection point with its green light.

3. Continue with the next collection points. Fuse the green energy body point with the red physical body collection point, then moving upward to fuse with the white universal collection point. Feel the energies fusing together above you.

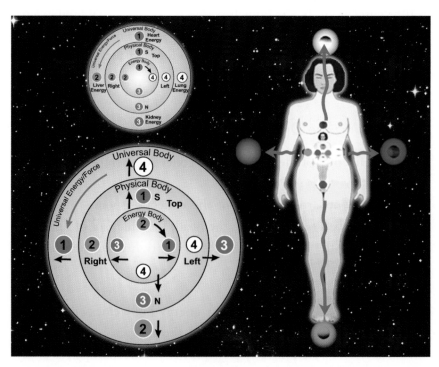

Fig. 6.30. Fuse inner positive energy with universal energy by turning the dial one position.

4. Moving to the right side, fuse the blue ball of the energy body collection point with the green ball of the physical body, and then move outward to fuse with the red ball of the universal collection point. Feel the energy fuse together at the right side.

5. Moving to the left, fuse the red ball of energy body light with the white ball of the physical body, then moving out to fuse with the blue ball of the universal collection point. Feel all these energies fuse together at the left.

6. Now bring the fusion process back inside the body: Take the fused light below you, drawing it first to the physical collection point and then into the energy body collection point. Bring the fused energy above the head down to the physical collection point and then into the energy body collection point (fig. 6.31).

7. Draw the fused energy from the right back to the physical body collection point and then to the energy body collection point.

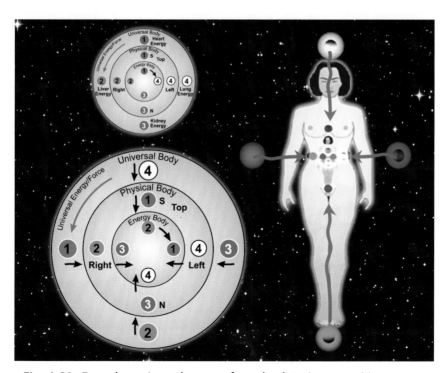

Fig. 6.31. Fuse the universal energy force back to inner positive energy and the energy body.

Draw the fused energy from the left back to the physical body collection point and then to the energy body collection point. Allow the four balls of fused energy to spiral around the cauldron. Let them increase in intensity and speed, going faster and faster, until they blend in the middle of the cauldron, forming the pearl.

8. Feel any residual energy spiral through the pakuas and fuse together into the cauldron, connecting with the brilliant pearl of white light. Feel the colors blend and fuse. This is where the alchemical process comes to life. At any time during the Fusion practice, if you feel the pearl you are working with is lost or diminished, simply become aware of the pakuas spiraling into the center of the cauldron.

9. Once you feel the form of the pearl, you can simply fuse the energy from inside of the energy body out to the physical and out to the universe and back, and there is no need to be aware of the different colors (fig. 6.32).

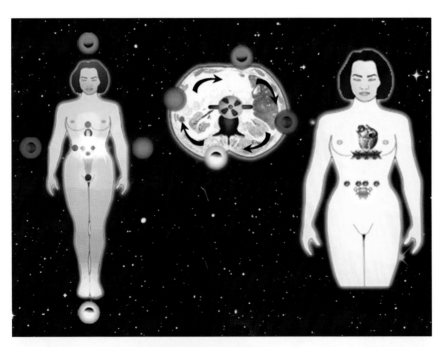

Fig. 6.32. Four fused energy balls spiral around the cauldron,
forming one energy pearl.

✿ Turning the Dial Again

Turn the dial one more station, clockwise for the energy body and counterclockwise for the universal body. Go through the steps of the meditation again—only the colors change—and then fuse from the energy body, to the physical body, to the universe and back, as four balls, spiraling faster and faster until fusing into one pearl (figs. 6.33–6.36).

Repeat the procedure using the four fused energy balls spiraling on top of the cauldron and forming one energy pearl (see fig. 6.37 on page 131).

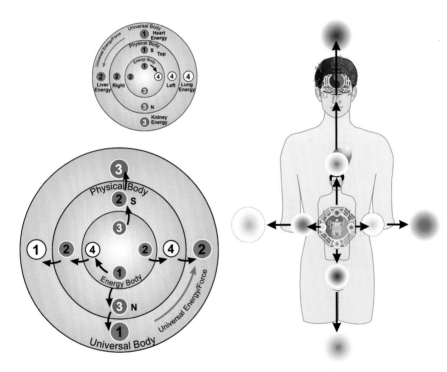

Fig. 6.33. Fuse inner positive energy with universal energy by turning the dial twice.

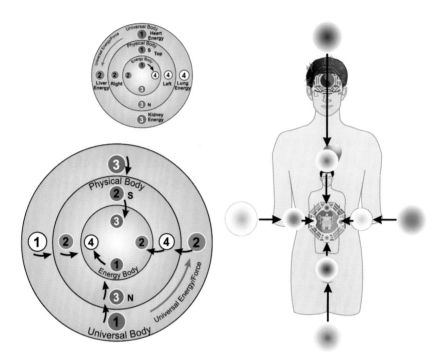

Fig. 6.34. Fuse the universal force back to the body and the energy body.

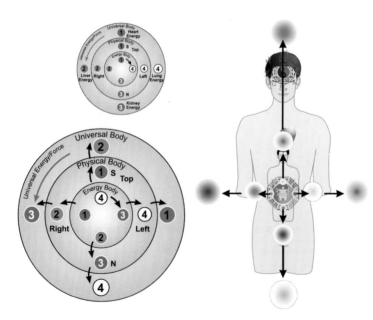

Fig. 6.35. Fuse inner positive energy with universal energy
by turning the dial a third time.

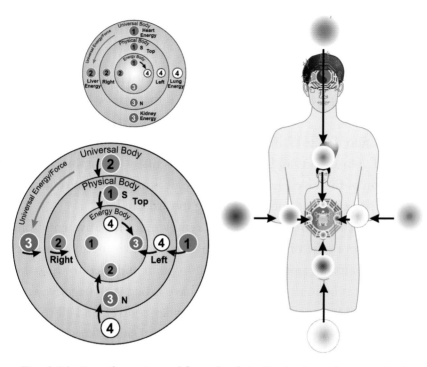

Fig. 6.36. Fuse the universal force back to the body and energy body.

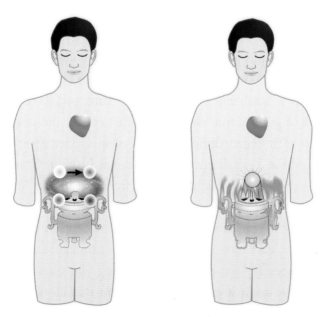

Fig. 6.37. Forming the cauldron and the pearl

THE FOUNDATION PRACTICE FOR
THE CREATION CYCLE

Here is an overview of the Fusion practices that help prepare you for the Creation Cycle, the advanced practice that you will learn in the next section.

1. The Inner Smile is the first step in connecting your consciousness to all your organs and glands. This is actually the first step of the Fusion of the Five Elements practice. It is important to remember how powerful and sublime smiling inward can be.

2. The next stage of practice is the removing of negative emotional energy from the organs. You bring the negative energy from each organ to its corresponding collection point and then to the pakua where it is neutralized. When you have brought all negative energies to all four pakuas and they are under control, and all residual energies have been brought to the back and side pakuas, the energies are then spiraled and compressed into the cauldron. There they form into the pearl of energy. As you collect the energies and direct their flow to the cauldron, you feel your center point illuminate with the bright light of the pearl.

3. Fuse the pearl to help activate virtue energy. Be aware of the energy body, physical body, and universal collection points; fuse them together outward and back to form the bigger pearl.

4. The pearl is capable of activating, attracting, and absorbing a great amount of good virtue energy. For this reason the pearl is circulated to each organ during the Creation Cycle. After practicing Fusion of the Five Elements, the pearl is brought from the cauldron to the perineum and is then circulated in the Microcosmic Orbit.

5. At this point you have a great awareness of each organ and the energy that each one is supplying. A continuation of this awareness is necessary for properly practicing the Creation Cycle of Cosmic Fusion. It is especially important that all negative energy has been removed and neutralized beforehand; otherwise, as the

virtue energy of the pearl increases, so will the negative energy, as you move the pearl through the Creation Cycle.

6. Therefore, in Fusion of the Five Elements practice, you remove the negative emotion of fear from the kidneys, by first listening to them, because the ears and kidneys have a connection. The removal of fear from the kidneys leaves room for the positive virtue of gentleness inherent in the kidneys to grow. And so on for the emotions of all the organs.

7. When you are ready to begin Cosmic Fusion, you bring the pearl to the heart to begin the Creation Cycle. The heart is the beginning point of this cycle because it is in the heart that compassion resides.

8. At the beginning of the Creation Cycle of Cosmic Fusion, you focus your smile on the virtues of joy, love, and happiness in the heart. You feel the virtues growing and purifying. It is important to develop genuine virtue here, not just one of those hail-fellow-well-met kind of things. You can spit out words like love, joy, and happiness without meaning them. But like the love that is mentioned in the Bible, 1 Corinthians 13, it has to be real and true; otherwise it is just a sounding brass or a tinkling cymbal. You have to flesh it out and breathe life into it.

9. Feel the unconditional love of the universe flowing down into the heart. With this combination of virtues—love, joy, happiness, unconditional love—you can definitely transform yourself, your organs, and those around you.

10. Let the positive heart energies of love, joy, and happiness activate the positive spleen energies of openness and fairness and centeredness. Blend this with the universal energy and feel the yellow light descending to the heart and spleen.

11. Let the positive heart energies of love, joy, and happiness activate the lung energies of courage, strength, and righteousness. Blend these energies with the universal energy and see the white light from above flow into the heart and lungs. Let the positive heart energies of love, joy, and happiness activate the kidney energies of

gentleness, softness, and calm in the kidneys. Blend both energies with universal energy and see the blue light coming down from above into the heart and kidneys.

12. Let the positive heart energies of love, joy, and happiness activate the liver energies of kindness, generosity, and benevolence. Blend these energies with universal energy and see the green light flowing from above into the heart and liver. You can do this meditation a few times.

13. Blend all the positive organ virtues in the heart, creating compassion energy. You may manifest this as a pearl. Move it in the Microcosmic Orbit, spiraling it from ten thousand to sixty thousand times a minute.

This completes the basic Fusion practices. These steps will be repeated through the rest of the formulas in the book. In the beginning it seems like a lot of work constructing all the pakuas, chanting, collecting the energy to fuse into the pearl. But once the formulas are set up, the whole process happens very quickly. It is not necessary to do all the steps every time. You might only want to chant a trigram one time instead of three. Remember, these extra steps are there to

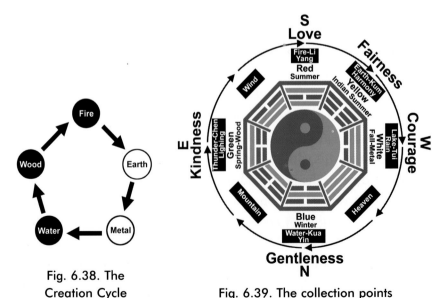

Fig. 6.38. The Creation Cycle

Fig. 6.39. The collection points

increase the strength of the pearl and expand your consciousness to connect with the universe. With this powerful pearl, it is time to begin Fusion II with the Creation Cycle.

 ## Begin Cosmic Fusion: The Creation Cycle

1. Activate the compassion fire and multi-orgasm energy and combine them together to connect with the universe.
2. Form the pearl through the fusion of energy from inside the body to the universe and from the universe back to the body, to spiral in the cauldron. Bring the pearl down to the perineum.
3. Feel the pearl connecting to the kidney energy.
4. Listen to the gentleness virtue of the kidneys.
5. The negative emotion of fear has already been removed from the kidneys. The energy remaining in the kidneys is their virtue energy—gentleness. Listen quietly to the gentleness of the kidneys, and be aware of the qualities of gentleness energy: cool, calm, blue, soft and silky, and tender. Enjoy these qualities. You can intensify them by concentrating on them. Bring the pearl from the perineum to the kidneys, and add the gentleness energy to the pearl. At any moment when you feel the pearl is weak, just form another pearl.
6. Now bring the pearl back to the kidneys' collection point at the perineum (see fig. 6.40 on the following page), where the gentleness will grow in intensity. All of the neutralized energy that is in the pearl now will take on the virtue energy of gentleness. Direct the pearl to the liver. Gentleness energy fuses with the kindness virtue of the liver.
7. Gentleness blends with kindness, the virtue of the liver. Look into the liver, connecting the eyes with the liver. Be aware of the kindness energy there. As you bring the pearl carrying the gentleness energy from the kidneys toward the liver, feel the gentleness energy activate and enhance the kindness energy. Enjoy the kindness energy. Feel the kindness intensify. Circulate the kindness energy in the liver. Its qualities can feel strong, round, smooth, soft, green, sweet and fragrant, warm and pleasant. You can feel satisfied.

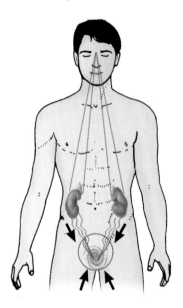
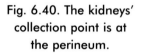

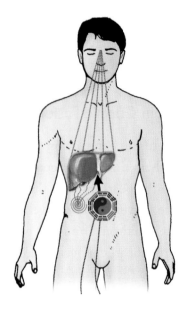

Fig. 6.40. The kidneys'
collection point is at
the perineum.

Fig. 6.41. The liver's
collection point is on the right
side at the level of the navel.

8. Absorb the kindness energy into the pearl, and bring the pearl to the liver collection point, at the level of the navel and in line with the right nipple (fig. 6.41). Here the combination of gentleness and kindness will intensify. Remember to relax and smile. Direct the pearl to the heart. Gentleness and kindness energy fuses with love, honor and respect, and joy in the heart.

9. Connect the tongue with the heart. Using your mind's eye and senses, allow the pearl, now consisting of gentleness and kindness, to flow up to the heart. Let the virtue energy of the pearl activate and enhance all the loving energy, joy and happiness, honor, respect, and peace in the heart. These good virtues of the heart can feel straight and open, bright red, warm, deep, calm, comfortable, and satisfying. Enjoy the virtuous feelings of the heart. The feeling will be different for each person as the energy blends. Feel the warmth and openness in the chest.

10. Let the pearl absorb the honor, respect, love, and joy. Bring the pearl down to the heart collection point behind the sternum (fig. 6.42). The pearl can now blend the virtue energies of the heart in a balanced way with the kindness and gentleness energies already within the pearl. Feel the collection point glowing. Then direct the pearl to the spleen/pancreas.

    Note for women: Women should be careful when the pearl is in the heart center. As a natural endowment, women tend to have more loving energy in the heart. When a woman loves she often forgets herself. This amount of love can heat up the heart center, and the practice can feel uncomfortable. It is best not to remain for too long in the heart if you feel uncomfortable.

11. Be aware of the connection of the mouth with the spleen/pancreas. As the pearl arrives at the spleen/pancreas, the honor and respect, love and joy energy that is now part of the pearl fuses with the spleen virtues of fairness and openness. The fairness and openness

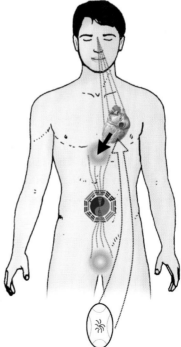

Fig. 6.42. The heart's collection point is behind the sternum. Blend the heart's loving energy with the kidneys' kindness energy in the pakua.

virtues of the spleen can feel expansive, clean, dry, bright yellow, smooth, warm, clear, and soft. Enjoy these feelings.

12. Let the pearl absorb the fairness and openness energy. Feel the pearl take on the qualities of the fairness and openness virtues in addition to the kindness, gentleness, honor, and respect virtues that already are present there. Bring the pearl to the spleen collection point behind the navel at the front pakua (fig. 6.43). Feel the fairness and openness energy intensify as it combines and blends with all the neutral and virtue energies already present in the pearl. Direct the pearl to the lungs.

13. Now the energy of fairness and openness fuses with the courage and righteousness virtues of the lungs. Connect the nose to both lungs. As the pearl arrives at the lungs, split the pearl into two pearls, one for each lung. The energy of fairness and openness that is now part of both pearls fuses and enhances the courage and righteousness energy of the lungs. When you feel righteous, you can feel tall, straight, uplifted, comfortable, strong, firm, proud, and satisfied. The energy can be fresh, bright, white, and pure. Enjoy the qualities of this energy.

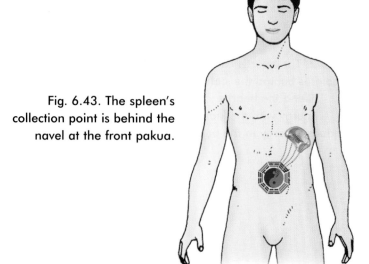

Fig. 6.43. The spleen's collection point is behind the navel at the front pakua.

14. Let the pearls absorb the courage and righteousness energy. Bring both pearls to the collection point of the lungs, at the level of the navel and in line with the left nipple (fig. 6.44). Feel the courage and righteousness energy intensify as it circulates in the lungs. Let the pearls blend these virtues with their kindness, gentleness, honor and respect, fairness and openness energies.

    Direct both pearls to both kidneys. Courage and righteousness fuse with gentleness: the cycle begins again at the kidneys.

15. As the pearls arrive at each kidney, the combined virtues of the pearls (especially the energy of courage and righteousness) enhance gentleness, and the cycle begins again. Repeat the cycle 2 more times. As you circulate the pearl in the second cycle, you will begin to notice that as the pearl arrives at each organ, the virtues will grow by themselves. Little by little, the energy will blend more evenly.

16. In the third cycle, bring the pearl from collection point to collection point without going into the organ first. With your attention

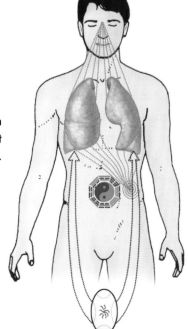

Fig. 6.44. The lungs' collection
point is on the left side at
the level of the navel.

on the collection point, the energy will flow into the organ without conscious effort, and will join with the virtue energy to flow back toward the collection point. In this way, the virtue energies are enhanced and increased each time you bring the pearl to a collection point. If you wish, you can practice the third round of the Creation Cycle 3 more times simply by bringing the pearl to the collection points. Each time you blend the energy, you increase it.

17. Your energy now begins to have the quality of an exquisite soup, with the proper combination of ingredients. Be aware of the quality of this energy. It is very special. Fuse all the good virtue energies into compassion energy. Creating a pearl of compassion energy requires a tremendous amount of purified energy. Compassion energy is not just love or kindness, gentleness or openness, but is a combination of all the good virtue energies, blended in proportion to become compassion energy. When you fuse the proportional blend of good virtue energy into a pearl of compassion energy, you will feel more centered. The energy of this pearl feels very different from the pearl you first formed.

18. When you feel the pearl of compassion energy strongly, move it down to the perineum. Using your mind and senses, begin to move all of the compassion energy through the Microcosmic Orbit, letting its bright pearl shine as it travels along. Feel the different quality of this energy. Be aware of the loving, comfortable, very beautiful way the organs feel as the energy runs through and spreads into them, filling them with life force energy. If you feel tired at any time, you can temporarily rest the pearl at your navel, and practice the Spinal Cord Breathing or the Inner Smile meditation. Return your concentration to the pearl to form it again, and return it to the Microcosmic Orbit for circulation. Move the pearl through the Microcosmic Orbit 9 to 18 times.

Shoot the Pearl above the Crown

1. As the pearl runs through the Microcosmic Orbit, begin to activate the cranial pump. Press your tongue to the palate, clench your teeth, pull back your chin, and roll your eyes up toward the crown (fig. 6.45). Feel the pulsing in your heart and in your head at the crown. You can touch your pulse at the wrist to increase your awareness of the pulse both at the wrist and the crown. Your mind also helps to activate the cranial pump.

2. Inhale, be aware of and squeeze the anus, and then exhale quickly to push the pearl up through the crown.

3. You might be aware of a light, beam, or frequency shooting out of your crown. This is the lead light first introduced in Fusion I. Sometimes it is called an indicator light because it will indicate

Fig. 6.45. Pull the eyes into their sockets. Roll the eyes up and look up to the crown.

how high up your pearl will be able to go. Just as a light is used to guide helicopters to their landing point, so will you use the lead light to guide the pearl back to the crown point.

4. Direct all of your senses to push the pearl up to the area 6 inches to 2 feet (15 to 60 centimeters) above your head. Move the pearl up and down, left and right.

5. Feel the universal force, the forces of the North Star and Big Dipper above your head, and the cosmic particle force in front of you, as they shine down to your pearl. Feel your pearl start to absorb this energy, and then feel it expand.

6. Bring your awareness to your feet. Feel the energy supplied to your whole body through your feet. This is the earth energy. The pearl continues to expand with all the energy coming to it from outside the physical body.

7. When you are ready, activate the cranial pump again. Press your tongue up, clench your teeth, pull back your chin, pull up your anus, and look up to the crown. Feel the beating in your heart and the pulse at your crown.

8. Activate the lead light, and let it shine up from your crown. It may feel like a certain energy frequency going out of the crown. Draw the pearl down to the lead light, and land the pearl. Inhale and draw the pearl down.

9. Circulate the pearl in the Microcosmic Orbit. Then bring it down to the navel and to the cauldron at the body's center. Collect the energy at the cauldron.

10. As you collect the energy and relax your mind, the pearl may disintegrate. Sometimes when you release the pearl, it vanishes. It is returning its energies, now enhanced by all the virtue energies and the outside forces, to the organs and glands. They become stronger and healthier each time you practice. Each time you gather the energy and form the pearl again, the pearl will be stronger.

Summary

Once you understand the practice and go through it a few times, there is no need to go through all the steps; you can just simply use the mind to recall the past experience. It becomes easier with practice. Trust and believe. Visualization turns into activation. Think, and let it happen.

Fusion I: Foundation Practices

1. Practice the Inner Smile, and activate compassion first (love and sexual energy combined).
2. Activate the three fires.
3. Create pakuas: front, back, facial, universal.
4. Form the cauldron, spin the pakuas.
5. Form organ collection points of the physical body, energy body, and universal body.
6. Remove negative energy from the organs.
7. Sense the colors of the collection points, using the imaginary dial for the pattern of colors.
8. Fuse the inner positive energy of the energy body and the physical body with the universal energy by turning the dial through stations 1, 2, and 3.
9. Fuse the universe energy back into the body and the energy body.
10. Create four balls of fused energy and spin them very very fast above the cauldron.
11. Form a pearl.

Begin Cosmic Fusion: The Creation Cycle

Be aware of the heart and cauldron activating the compassion fire.

1. Listen to the gentleness virtue of the kidneys.
2. Gentleness energy activates the kindness virtue of the liver.

3. Kindness energy activates honor, respect, and love in the heart.
4. The energy of honesty and respect activates the fairness and openness virtues of the spleen/pancreas.
5. The energy of fairness and openness activates the courage and righteousness virtues of the lungs.
6. Courage and righteousness enhance gentleness: the cycle begins again at the kidneys.
7. Combine all good virtue energies into the heart and create compassion energy.
8. Move the compassion energy through the Microcosmic Orbit.
9. Shoot the pearl above the crown.
10. Practice Chi Massage.

Opening the Thrusting Channels

We have come to the point in our practice where the positive emotional energy of the organs has been absorbed into the pearl. We can now begin to circulate the pearl energy in four of the eight special channels: the Governor and Functional Channels (which make up the Microcosmic Orbit), the Thrusting Channels (or Routes), and the Belt Channels (or Routes). The three Thrusting Routes run vertically through the center of the body, linking the chakra centers. The Belt Routes spiral around the body, strengthening the aura and providing a form of psychic self-defense. This chapter in the Cosmic Fusion practice involves opening these three Thrusting Channels.

THEORY OF THE THRUSTING CHANNELS

The Thrusting Channels are a powerful means to clean out negative emotions and detoxify the organs and glands. If you utilize them in this way, the three Thrusting Channels will serve as strong and efficient ways to monitor your center and observe the status of your emotions.

The Thrusting Channels run from the perineum to the crown and are separately identified as the Middle, Left, and Right Thrusting Channels. The Middle Thrusting Channel begins directly at the

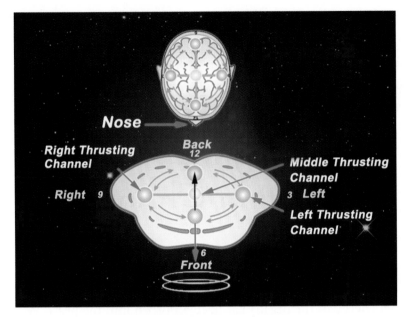

Fig. 7.1. The Thrusting Channels

perineum and runs vertically up to the crown. The Left Thrusting Channel is located $1^1/_2$ to 3 inches to the left of the Middle Channel, while the Right Thrusting Channel is $1^1/_2$ to 3 inches to its right (fig. 7.1).

When you are feeling emotional, you can check the Thrusting Channels, especially the Middle Channel, to discern whether you are off center. You will know you are out of balance when you feel the emotions running more on the left or the right side, instead of through the middle of the body. If you center the emotions through the Middle Thrusting Channel, and balance the Left and Right Thrusting Channels, you will very quickly center yourself. The Thrusting Channels serve as guidelines to balanced decision making in your daily life.

PROCEDURE FOR OPENING THE THRUSTING CHANNELS

The Thrusting Channels need the tremendous energy of good virtue to help them open. Begin by forming a pearl of virtue energy. With your continued, conscientious practice of the compassion fire and the fusion of the inside with the universal energy to form the pearl, you will be able to assimilate the energies into a new and stronger pearl, a pearl that responds to your intention. This means that all you need do to form a new pearl is to concentrate on the cauldron and the pearl in it, and on the front, back, left, and right pakuas, and to fuse inside with the outside energy. Control of your internal weather, your senses, organs, and emotions, will be possible in as little as a few seconds.

Although you do not have to go through all the steps of chanting and collecting the energies every time you do the Fusion practice, taking these steps is helpful and creates a stronger experience. Thus, the first steps to opening the Thrusting Channels are to construct the pakuas; chant the eight directions; form the collection points of the physical body, the energy body, and the universal body; and fuse them together into the pearl.

You will then thrust up the pearl from the perineum (or the testicles, in men). Each Thrusting Channel precisely penetrates the body.

Although it may seem difficult at first, using your beautiful pearl will help make it easier. Other aids, such as pulling up the anus and inhaling, help the energy move in each of the three channels. Once you are able to pass the energy through the channels, you will find that the energy moves by itself without assistance.

Note: You must be very careful and gentle with this procedure. If the energy reaches the heart and head too quickly through the Thrusting Channels, the heart may become congested and you may experience pressure. If the heart becomes congested and overheats with energy: 1) Do not thrust above the diaphragm, and 2) Practice the heart sound (haw-w-w-w-w-w). Do not overheat the heart, liver, or head.

Initially, the Thrusting Channels have a diameter of approximately $1/2$ to 1 inch. Once they are activated, they can become very wide. At first, concern yourself with drawing the energy directly up. Later, when you have become familiar with the process, you can spiral the energy up each route.

Practice from a Seated Position

Like many other Universal Tao exercises, we practice the methods of opening the Thrusting Channels from a seated position. Sitting on a chair with your feet touching the floor and your spine erect connects you with two important energy "wires": earth energy and universal (or heavenly) energy. The energy body you eventually create needs the ground wire of earth energy to hold and support it. Otherwise, you can become disoriented and lost. Once you are more in control of the energy, you can practice while standing, or while lying down on a bed or the floor.

The Anal Muscle

The Universal Tao system requires that you have a strong anal muscle. If you do not strengthen your anal muscle, you will not progress very far in any of the Universal Tao practices. The anal muscle is connected to the perineum and everything in the body above it (fig. 7.2). Think of the anus and perineum as your foundation. If you were to invest all of your money on building the top floors of a building, and never invested anything in the foundation, the building would fall. The anus

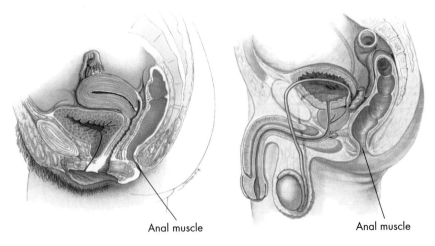

Anal muscle   Anal muscle

Fig. 7.2. Anal muscle

muscle is used to seal your "lower gate." Closing this orifice helps to retain and prevent loss of your energy.

The Saliva

Saliva is another aid in performing these exercises. Once you have been able to bring the energy up through all the routes to the crown successfully, saliva generation becomes very important.

In the body, the moon influences the kidneys, which are linked with the salivary glands (fig. 7.3), the ovaries, and semen. When the kidneys are stimulated during sex, the chi rises up through the spine and then flows down in the saliva, and the kidneys' essence transforms into sexual energy. In addition to its role in the digestive process, the saliva has other functions: purifying the mouth, and nourishing the water of life, our immortality. The energy from the saliva lubricates one hundred joints, and it stimulates and harmonizes the organs. It is very important to enhance the production of saliva by absorbing the moon's energy through the breath absorption exercises. It is a sign that the techniques are working when the saliva floods into the mouth.

Although saliva is a lubricant for the channels, it first serves as an agent to burn and clean any impurities out of them that could block

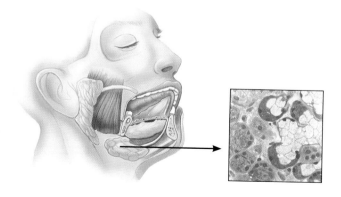

Fig. 7.3. The salivary glands

the flow of energy. So, when resting during the practice of opening the thrusting channels, move your tongue around to create saliva. Make it thick and swallow it forcefully, feeling it go down the channels that you are working on.*

Perceptions and Patterns

Each person experiences the Thrusting Channels according to his or her own kinesthetic or visual perceptions. The majority of people are more kinesthetic and can undeniably feel the quality of the condensed energy as it passes through each level of the channels.

Visual people can see patterns and colors. The Thrusting Channels, like the organs they intersect, have corresponding colors. The Left Channel is red; the Middle is white; and the Right is blue. Regardless of your perceptual tendency, you will use both the senses and the organs to control the Thrusting Channels.

The denser or more polluted the organ, the more energy it requires to pass through the affected Thrusting Channel. As a safety precaution and as a preparation for the ability to move the energy and to prevent it from sticking, we open the Thrusting Channels in four stages. We bring the pearl:

1. Up to the diaphragm
2. Up to the neck
3. Up to and out of the crown
4. Down to the feet, into the ground, around and up to the crown

We do this a total of 9 times at each stage, in the following sequence: 1) left, 2) middle, 3) right, 4) middle, 5) left, 6) middle, 7) right, 8) middle, and 9) left.

---

*For more information on the saliva, see Mantak Chia, *Golden Elixir Chi Kung* (Rochester, Vt.: Destiny Books, 2005).

Men and Women Practice with Channels Differently

Once the channels have been completely opened, men and women practice differently (fig. 7.4). Without stopping, men will thrust the energy directly up through the Thrusting Channels and out of the crown. They then will bring the energy back in to flow down the Thrusting Channels and down through the soles of the feet into the ground. They can continue to bring the flow up around the body and in through the crown.

Without stopping, women will thrust the energy down through the soles of the feet into the ground, and then up through the Thrusting Channels to and out of the crown. They then allow the energy to spray down around the body, tuck it under their feet and draw it back in through the toes.

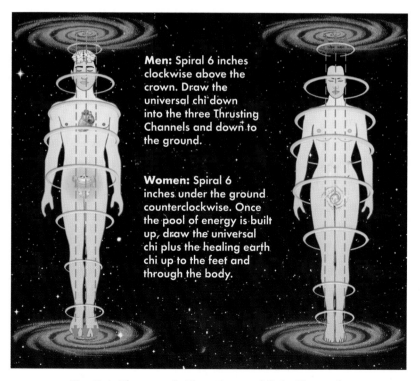

Men: Spiral 6 inches clockwise above the crown. Draw the universal chi down into the three Thrusting Channels and down to the ground.

Women: Spiral 6 inches under the ground counterclockwise. Once the pool of energy is built up, draw the universal chi plus the healing earth chi up to the feet and through the body.

Fig. 7.4. The cosmic Thrusting and Belt Channels

Opening the Thrusting Channels

Form a Pearl and Send It to the Perineum

1. From a seated position, smile down to your organs and glands, and put yourself in a state of relaxation and happiness. Begin with the meditation exercises of the Creation Cycle to form a pearl of compassion energy.

   As you have learned, there are many steps in forming such a pearl. However, once you have programmed yourself to all of these steps through continued practice, you can simply push the button and the whole program is activated. When you are able simply to sit quietly and feel the sensation of compassion energy forming, you are pushing the button, and the entire process takes very little time. In other words once you have experienced compassion energy, all you need to do is to recall the state in order to create the energy again. You will not need to go through the entire process each time. You will know by looking at the pearl whether or not the process has been completed. If you find something is not right, you can review the steps and find out where the problem is.

2. As the pearl is forming, use your mind and senses to control it. Slowly move it down to the perineum. At any time during your practice, if the pearl seems to weaken or diminish, or you lose track of it, return to the navel and quickly form a new pearl. Bring that pearl to the perineum and resume practice.

While you are learning how to bring the energy up through the channels, it is easier to focus on the organs the channel passes through than to focus on the channel itself. You might think of the process as learning how to read. Once you are able to read, you no longer have to think about your ABC's.

🌀 Stage One: The Thrusting Channels to below the Diaphragm

In all Universal Tao practices, it is important to train the power of the mind and senses to control our energy (chi). The power of mind, eye, and heart guides the chi, providing a way to control and direct your life force. Breathing techniques also help to activate the Thrusting Channels. It is necessary to have some control over independent breathing through each nostril. Since in the beginning this is difficult to do, you can use your right index finger to cover the right nostril. Feel the breath on the left side only. Use the left eye, ear, and nostril to assist you in drawing up the energy.

⭘ The Left Thrusting Channel to the Diaphragm

- *The Left Testicle (Men), Left Ovary (Women), and Left Kidney*

1. Sit up, using your mind, heart, and eye power to look inside and be aware of the perineum. Also become aware of your left nostril, left ear, left eye, and left side of your anus (figs. 7.5 and 7.6).

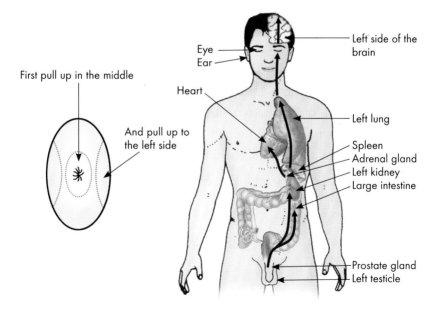

Fig. 7.5. The male Left Thrusting Channel

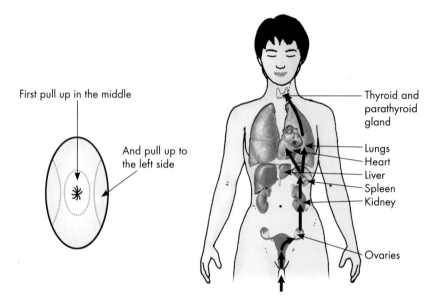

First pull up in the middle

And pull up to the left side

Thyroid and parathyroid gland

Lungs
Heart
Liver
Spleen
Kidney

Ovaries

Fig. 7.6. The female Left Thrusting Channel

2. Activate the Left Thrusting Channel by inhaling through the left nostril in short sips (about 10 percent of lung capacity with each breath).

3. Then, men slightly pull the left testicle and the left side of the anus up toward the left. Women slightly pull the left side of the anus up toward the left. Draw the pearl up with each sip of air. The left eye should look down internally. Use the mind/eye power to look up as the pearl is drawn up. (The physical eyes do not actually look up.) Women direct the pearl to the left ovary and the left kidney; men direct the pearl to the left kidney.

4. Exhale, relax the eye and the muscles, letting the pearl drop to the left side of the anus (and left testicle in men), and rest. Rest and feel the left side become lighter as the energy begins to flow up without effort. Practice 9 times. Each time you rest use your mind to trace the Left Thrusting Channel.

- *Spleen*

1. Close the right nostril, inhale, and pull up. As you sip in the air, use the mind power and the left eye, ear, and nostril to draw the

energy up from the left testicle (men), through the left ovary (women), the left kidney, and up to the spleen.

2. Exhale; release the energy down. Practice 9 times. Rest, and feel the energy flow up the Left Thrusting Channel to the spleen, under the diaphragm.

○ The Middle Thrusting Channel to the Diaphragm

● *Prostate (Men) or Cervix (Women)*

Men concentrate on the middle of the scrotum, perineum, and anus (see fig. 7.7 on the following page). Women concentrate on the middle of the perineum and anus (see fig. 7.8 on the following page).

1. Inhale, and pull up the middle of the scrotum (men), perineum, and anus. Use all the senses to draw the energy up to the prostate (men) or cervix (women). Look up with both eyes as you do so.
2. Relax the eyes and anal muscle, and let the pearl drop back down to the perineum and scrotum (men). Feel the energy begin to flow up as you rest. Do this 9 times.

● *The Small/Large Intestine, Aorta, and Vena Cava*

1. Inhale and pull up the scrotum (men) and anus. Use the eyes, ears, and nose to draw the energy to the prostate/cervix, small intestine, large intestine, aorta, and vena cava. Do not thrust beyond the diaphragm.
2. Rest, and feel the energy flow up through the Middle Thrusting Channel to the vena cava.
3. Practice 9 times.

● *The Stomach and Pancreas*

1. Follow the above procedure, and thrust through the middle organs to the stomach and pancreas.
2. Practice 9 times.
3. Swallow the saliva, rest, and feel the energy flow in the Middle Thrusting Channel up to the diaphragm.

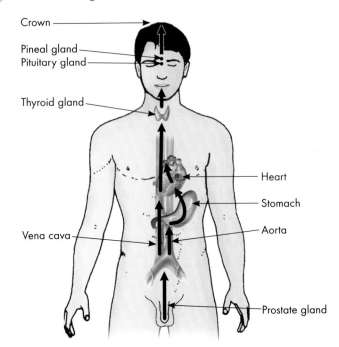

Fig. 7.7. The male Middle Thrusting Channel

Crown — Pineal gland — Pituitary gland — Thyroid gland — Heart — Stomach — Vena cava — Aorta — Prostate gland

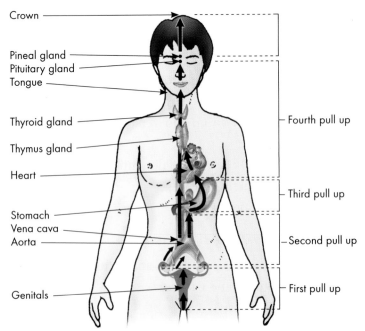

Fig. 7.8. The female Middle Thrusting Channel

Crown — Pineal gland — Pituitary gland — Tongue — Thyroid gland — Thymus gland — Heart — Stomach — Vena cava — Aorta — Genitals — Fourth pull up — Third pull up — Second pull up — First pull up

⭘ The Right Thrusting Channel to the Diaphragm

● *The Right Testicle (Men), Right Ovary (Women) and Right Kidney*

1. Close the left nostril with the index finger of the left hand. Use the right eye, ear, and nostril to direct the energy up the right channel. Put your right hand on the right kidney.

2. Inhale in short sips equal to 10 percent of lung capacity. Look up with the right eye. Pull up the right testicle (men) and the right muscle of the anus toward the right side. Direct the energy up the Right Thrusting Channel to the right ovary (women) and kidney.

3. Exhale and rest. Practice 9 times. Let the pearl drop down, returning to the perineum and right testicle (men). Feel the right side become lighter as the energy flows up the Right Thrusting Channel to the right kidney without effort (figs. 7.9 and 7.10).

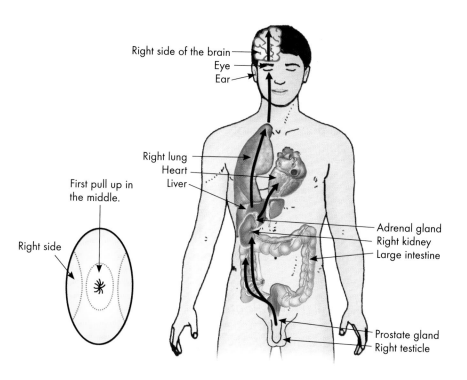

Fig. 7.9. The male Right Thrusting Channel

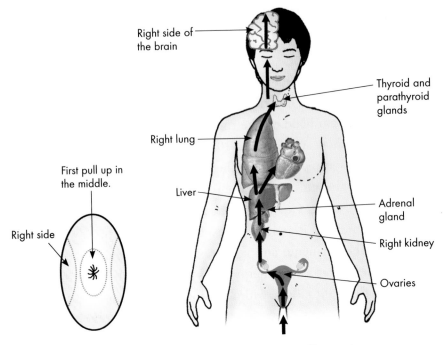

Right side of the brain

Thyroid and parathyroid glands

Right lung

First pull up in the middle.

Liver

Adrenal gland

Right side

Right kidney

Ovaries

Fig. 7.10. The female Right Thrusting Channel

- *The Liver*

1. Close the left nostril, inhale, and pull up. Using the right eye, ear, and nostril, draw the energy up from the right testicle (men), through the right ovary (women), the right kidney, and up to the liver.

2. Exhale, relax, and let the pearl return to the perineum. Practice 9 times.

3. Rest, and feel the flow of energy through the Right Thrusting Channel to the liver, under the diaphragm.

❂ Combine All Three Routes

Continue to practice moving the pearl up and down, from the perineum to under the diaphragm, through a combination of all three Thrusting Channels in the following sequence of 9 steps, until the energy is flowing easily: 1) left channel; 2) middle channel; 3) right channel; 4) middle; 5) left; 6) middle; 7) right; 8) middle; and 9) left. It helps to quicken the speed with each attempt.

Note: Stay relaxed during this exercise, and avoid using force. Once you are accustomed to thrusting the pearl and feel that the channels are clear, there is no need to close the nostrils for the left and right channels. Just simply pull up the perineum and anus, and use the power of the mind.

🌀 Clear the Routes with Saliva

1. Prepare the saliva. First sweep your tongue across the outer surface of your upper teeth, starting on the left side at your wisdom tooth, with the tip of the tongue going along the gums. When you arrive at your upper right wisdom tooth, move the tip of your tongue down to the lower right wisdom tooth, and sweep it along the front of the lower teeth.
2. When you arrive at the lower left wisdom tooth, start again at the upper wisdom tooth. Circle around in this manner a few times.
3. Then similarly sweep along the inner surface of the upper and lower teeth and gums. Your mouth will begin to fill with saliva.
4. Gather the saliva into a ball using your tongue. Press your tongue to the roof of your mouth and swallow the saliva quickly with a gulping action. Feel the saliva burn out the impurities in the channels and lubricate them.

Practice this stage for about one or two weeks until you can control the energy very well. Then continue to the next stage. Each time you finish, move the energy in the Microcosmic Orbit and collect the energy in the cauldron. When you are ready to continue to the next stage, practice Spinal Cord Breathing at this point in your preparation. (See the Universal Tao book *Awaken Healing Light of the Tao* for instructions on Spinal Cord Breathing.)

◕ *Stage Two: The Thrusting Channels to the Neck*

◯ **The Left Thrusting Channel to the Neck**

● *The Diaphragm*

Using the procedure already described, bring the pearl up the Left Thrusting Channel to below the diaphragm, and let it return down to the perineum.

● *Left Thyroid and Parathyroid Glands*

1. Using the same procedure, bring the pearl up through the left ovary (women), left kidney, and spleen, and continue to bring the pearl up to the left lung, and left thyroid and parathyroid glands.
2. Hold for a while, and then exhale. Let the pearl return to the perineum.
3. Practice 9 times. Be aware of the energy flow up to the neck through the Left Thrusting Channel.

◯ **The Middle Thrusting Channel to the Neck**

● *The Diaphragm*

Using the procedure described, bring the pearl up the Middle Thrusting Channel to below the diaphragm, and let it return down to the perineum.

● *Thymus, Thyroid, and Parathyroid Glands*

1. Using the same procedure, bring the pearl up from the perineum through the prostate (men), cervix (women), small/large intestine, aorta and vena cava, stomach, and pancreas.
2. Continue to bring the pearl up to the heart, to the thymus gland under the sternum, and up to the middle of the neck, the thyroid and parathyroid glands.
3. Exhale, relax, and let the pearl drop down again. Practice 9 times. Be aware of the Middle Thrusting Channel as the energy flows up to the neck.

O **The Right Thrusting Channel to the Neck**

● *The Diaphragm*

Using the procedure described, bring the pearl up the Right Thrusting Channel to below the diaphragm, and let it return down to the perineum.

● *The Right Thyroid and Parathyroid Glands*

1. Using the same procedure, bring the pearl up from the perineum to the right ovary (women), right kidney, liver, and continue to bring the pearl up to the right lung, and to the right thyroid and parathyroid glands.
2. Exhale, and slowly release the energy down.
3. Practice 9 times. Be aware of the Right Thrusting Channel as the energy flows up to the neck.

Combine the Three Routes and Clear with Saliva

Practice all three Thrusting Channels to the neck, 9 times each, in the same sequence as delineated for the diaphragm: left, middle, right, middle, left, middle, right, middle, and left.

If your throat feels dry, you can collect and warm the saliva in your mouth. Tighten your neck a little bit, and swallow the saliva with a guttural sound down to the stomach. Feel the saliva like a fire clearing all three channels.

Practice this stage for about one or two weeks, each time finishing by moving the pearl in the Microcosmic Orbit and collecting it in the cauldron. End by resting and concentrating on all three channels, visualizing the left route as red, the middle as white, and the right as blue.

Stage Three: The Thrusting Channels to the Crown

In stage three of Opening the Thrusting Channels, the pearl is thrust through the channels up to and out of the crown.

○ The Left Thrusting Channel to the Crown

● *The Left Eye*

Follow the procedure already described for thrusting through the Left Thrusting Channel to the neck, and continue thrusting to the left eye.

● *The Crown*

1. Repeat the Left Thrusting Channel to the left eye, and continue to thrust the pearl up through the left hemisphere of the brain to the crown.
2. Practice 9 times.
3. Rest, and mentally trace the Left Thrusting Channel from the perineum to the crown.

○ The Middle Thrusting Channel to the Crown

● *The Mid-eyebrow*

Repeat the Middle Thrusting Channel procedure as described to the neck, and continue thrusting to the mid-eyebrow.

● *The Crown*

1. Repeat the Middle Thrusting Channel to the mid-eyebrow, and continue to thrust the pearl up through the pituitary gland to the pineal gland at the crown.
2. Practice 9 times.
3. Rest, and mentally trace the entire Middle Thrusting Channel.

○ The Right Thrusting Channel to the Crown

● *The Right Eye*

Repeat the Right Thrusting Channel procedure as described to the neck, and continue thrusting to the right eye.

- *The Crown*

1. Repeat the Right Thrusting Channel to the right eye, and continue thrusting the pearl up to the right hemisphere of the brain and then to the crown.
2. Practice 9 times.
3. Rest, and trace the route mentally from the perineum to the crown.

Continue to Practice the Three Thrusting Channels to the Crown

Continue to practice the three Thrusting Channels to the crown 9 times in the same sequence as was delineated for the diaphragm and again for the neck: left, middle, right, middle, left, middle, right, middle, and left (fig. 7.11).

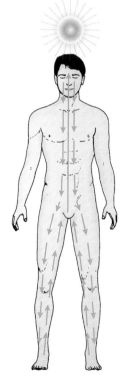

Fig. 7.11. The three
Thrusting Channels taking
energy up to the crown

You now have succeeded in bringing the pearl through the Thrusting Channels to the crown. Your goal is to follow the sequence above, using nine thrusts distributed among these three channels. Be aware of how and where the energy flows through the three Thrusting Channels, and how the three channels penetrate all the organs and glands. These channels are very powerful. They clean, detoxify, and purify the organs at a much deeper level.

⚛ Bring the Pearl into the Microcosmic Orbit

When you have finished this stage of practice, you can bring the pearl into the Microcosmic Orbit and circulate it. Feel the Microcosmic Orbit encircling the Thrusting Channels. The top and bottom of the Thrusting Channels are joined with the Microcosmic Orbit at the crown and the perineum. Use your mind to assist the flow of energy through the Thrusting Channels and through the Microcosmic Orbit when the pearl reaches the crown point or the perineum point.

Your Microcosmic Orbit practice changes dramatically after you learn the Fusion meditations. When you first practiced the Microcosmic Orbit, the energy you moved through your channels was raw energy. By contrast, when you reach the level of Fusion practice, the energy is more refined and condensed, and therefore much more powerful. The Fusion practice includes the Microcosmic Orbit, so it might be said that the Fusion meditation is simply a more advanced way of practicing the Microcosmic Orbit meditation. Practice this stage for two or three weeks until you feel you have gained control of the energy.

⚛ Extending the Three Thrusting Channels above the Crown

Once we have purified and transformed the negative energy of the organs back into usable life force energy (Fusion of the Five Elements), distilled this energy along with the virtue chi of the organs into the pearl (Cosmic Fusion), and opened all our reservoirs or special channels, giving us a larger energy capacity, we can increase our virtue energies further by connecting with the external sources of Five Elements chi and directing the external chi toward its associated organs. Moving the pearl out of the physical body makes it easier for the pearl to absorb these energies. It becomes like an antenna that receives the external chi and conducts it into the physical body. In this way, we again nourish our health in this life as well as strengthening the energy body and spirit in preparation for the next (fig. 7.12).

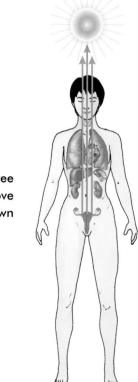

Fig. 7.12. The three Thrusting Channels above the crown

After you gain full control of the energy, you will be able to send the pearl out of the body at the crown. Begin to develop the ability to form a fresh pearl quickly, by practicing fusion of the physical energy and energy body, out to the universal energy and back in again to form the pearl. Follow with the Creation Cycle. Then, thrust the pearl up through the Thrusting Channels to quickly clear out these routes. You are now ready to extend the channels above the crown.

Bring the energy down to the perineum, and start with the Left Thrusting Channel up to the left side of the crown. Push the pearl out at the crown of the head to a height of about 3 to 6 inches (7 1/2 to 15 centimeters) above the crown. Similarly, push the pearl out of the crown through the Middle Thrusting Channel, and then the Right Thrusting Channel (fig. 7.13).

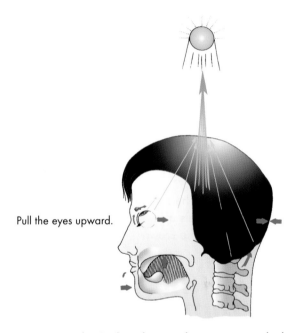

Pull the eyes upward.

Fig. 7.13. Use physical and mental power to push the pearl of energy up through the crown.

Each time you push the pearl out at the crown, be aware of an energy ball hovering about 6 to 10 inches (15 to 25 centimeters) above the crown. Draw and absorb the universal energy into the pearl. Then slowly let the energy melt and flow down to the crown, and then into the body, all the way down through the three Thrusting Channels to the perineum.

🌀 *Stage Four: The Leg Routes of the Thrusting Channels into the Ground*

In the final stage of opening the Thrusting Channels, you will have the energy go all the way down to the feet, into the ground, and then up through the channels, with each thrust (fig. 7.14). After you have formed another new pearl by practicing Fusion I and the Creation Cycle of Fusion II, bring the energy down to the perineum.

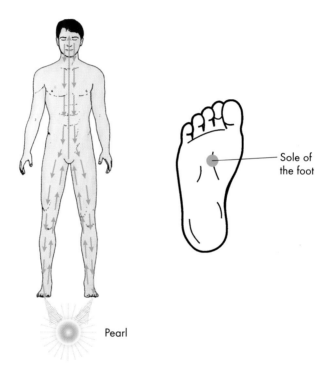

Sole of the foot

Pearl

Fig. 7.14. The three Thrusting Channels taking energy down to the ground

◎ Bring the Energy Down to the Soles of the Feet

● *The Left Thrusting Channel*

1. Split the pearl in two, and bring the energy from the perineum down the back of both legs to the backs of the knees, and then down to the heels and soles of the feet. Stop for a while, and absorb the earth energy through the soles.

2. Then bring the energy up the front of the legs through the big toes, knees, front of the thighs, all the way back to the perineum.

3. Recombine the pearl at the perineum. Then run the energy through the Left Thrusting Channel by slightly tightening the left side of the anus and looking up with the left eye.

4. Bring the pearl all the way up through the left hemisphere of the brain and left crown, and out to about 3 inches (7½ centimeters) above the crown.

5. Relax, and bring the pearl down to the perineum.

- *The Middle Thrusting Channel*

1. From the perineum, split the pearl, and bring the pearl down the backs of both legs to the soles of both feet. Absorb the earth energy through the soles, then move the energy up to the toes, to the knees, returning to the perineum.

2. Recombine the pearl at the perineum. Now bring the pearl all the way up the Middle Thrusting Channel, squeezing the middle of the anus and looking up with both eyes.

3. Bring the pearl all the way up through all the organs and glands to the crown, and out to about 3 inches (7½ centimeters) above the crown. Then bring it down to the perineum again.

- *The Right Thrusting Channel*

1. From the perineum, split the pearl, and bring it down the backs of both legs. Absorb the earth energy through the soles of the feet. Then bring the pearl up again to the perineum.

2. Recombine the pearl at the perineum. Use the right anus muscle, look up with the right eye, and bring the pearl all the way up the Right Thrusting Channel through the right hemisphere of the brain and out of the crown 3 inches (7½ centimeters.) Bring it down to the perineum.

Continue bringing the pearl to the Thrusting Channels in the following sequence: left, middle, right, middle, left, middle, right, middle, and left, finishing each step by looping the pearl through the leg route. End on the left side of the perineum. Swallow the saliva, as described earlier.

- *Bring the Energy into the Ground*

Once you have practiced bringing the pearl down to the soles of the feet for a while, add a new step.

1. Begin by shooting the energy from the perineum down the backs of the legs and through the soles of the feet, from 6 inches to 1 foot into the ground.
2. Feel a connection or rooting to the earth, then draw the energy up to the soles of the feet, to the toes, up the front of the legs, and into the Thrusting Channels.

With this step you have completed opening all the Thrusting Channels. Practice for two or three weeks until you develop full control of the energy traveling through these channels.

Men and Women Now Practice Differently

At this stage, all the Thrusting Channels and Leg Routes are open, and men and women start to practice differently. Both quickly practice Fusion I, and the Creation Cycle and Thrusting Channels of Fusion II, and bringing the pearl to the perineum.

Men Start by Bringing the Pearl to the Crown

1. Men bring the pearl from the perineum up to and out of the crown to about 6 inches (15 centimeters). Feel your pearl hook up with the higher energy source, the heavenly energy.
2. Absorb this energy into the pearl. Then bring the energy back into the body. As it enters the crown, let the pearl split in three. Feel the energy penetrate through three holes at the top of the head. Feel it flowing back down to the perineum through the three Thrusting Channels, penetrating all the organs and glands (see fig. 7.15 on the following page).

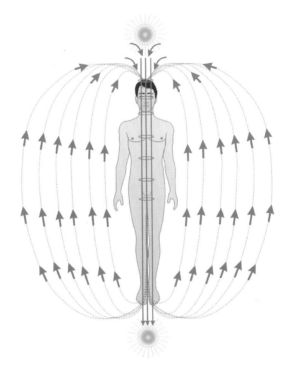

Fig. 7.15. Men bring the pearl to the crown first;
then send the energy back down through the body.

3. From the perineum, men will push and guide the energy down the back of both legs to the soles of the feet, and then 6 to 12 inches (15 to 30 centimeters) into the ground. Feel a connection or rooting to the earth, then draw the earth energy up to the soles of the feet. Bring the energy to the toes. Start to spread the energy out from the ten toes, shooting the energy up to and into the crown, like a waterfall with a reverse flow. Draw the pearl back down to the perineum, and then repeat the process.

4. Practice 9 times. Feel the flow of energy like a magnetic field surrounding your body.

○ Women Start by Bringing the Pearl to the Feet

1. Women bring the pearl down to the perineum, divide it, and shoot it down the backs of both legs, through the soles of the

feet, 6 to 12 inches (15 to 30 centimeters) into the ground.

2. Feel a connection or rooting to the earth, and absorb the earth energy into the pearl. Then draw the earth energy up to the soles of the feet. Bring the energy all the way up the front of the legs, to the knees and back to the perineum. As the energy travels up the legs, feel it penetrate the bones.

3. Spread the energy into the three Thrusting Channels, and thrust it as though it were on a three-lane highway all the way up to the crown. Feel the energy spread from the crown like a spring or water fountain pouring out of and around the body, entering into the soles of the feet, where it again joins together with energy from the earth. While the energy is outside and circling the body, it is also gathering pure, radiant cosmic energy (fig. 7.16).

4. Repeat this meditation 9 times.

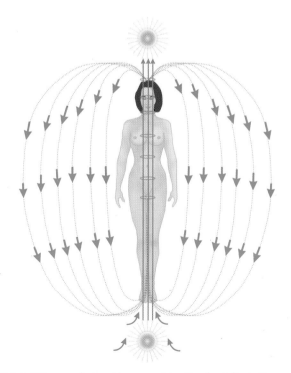

Fig. 7.16. Women bring the pearl to the feet first; then send the energy back up through the body.

☯ *Finishing the Meditation*

Both men and women should finish by collecting the energy at the cauldron and practicing Chi Massage. This completes the practice of the Thrusting Channels. Continue to practice for a few weeks until you gain control of it.

☯ Additional Exercise for Opening the Thrusting Channels

☯ *Alternate Nostril Breathing*

The alternate nostril breathing helps to generate more power in moving the pearl up and down the Thrusting Channels. By closing one side of the nose, it is easier to move the pearl through the specific left or right channel (fig. 7.17).

Fig. 7.17. Alternate nostril breathing

1. Hold the right nostril closed with the finger tips.
2. Inhale up through the left nostril, and feel the pearl move up from the perineum to the crown.
3. Exhale out through the left nostril and bring the pearl back down to the perineum.
4. Inhale through the left nostril and bring the pearl to the middle of the perineum.
5. Close both nostrils and suck the pearl up through the Middle Thrusting Channel to the crown. This suction is created by an inhaling motion without actually drawing any air into the lungs.
6. Hold the right arm down toward the ground and exhale any cloudy or gray energy out of the Thrusting Channel (fig. 7.18).
7. Now repeat the same procedure in the Right Thrusting Channel. Hold the left nostril closed with the fingertips.
8. Inhale up through the right nostril, and feel the pearl move up from the perineum to the crown.
9. Exhale out through the right nostril and bring the pearl back down to the perineum.

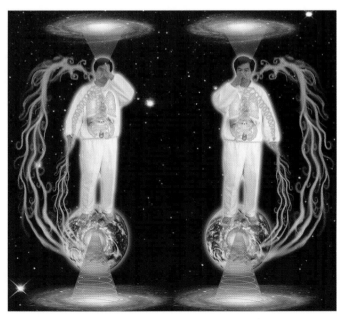

Fig. 7.18. Exhale cloudy energy out of the Thrusting Channel.

10. Inhale through the right nostril and bring the pearl to the middle of the perineum.
11. Close both nostrils and suck the pearl up through the Middle Thrusting Channel to the crown.
12. Hold the left arm out and down to the ground, exhaling any cloudy gray energy down to the earth.
13. Repeat 3 to 9 times or until you feel the Thrusting Channels clean and clear with positive energy (fig. 7.19).

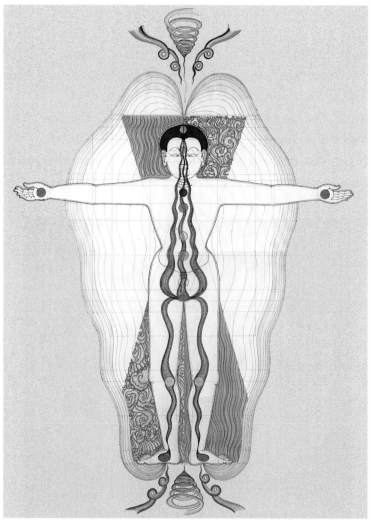

Fig. 7.19. The Thrusting Channels

Summary: Opening the Thrusting Channels

Begin the Fusion practice by opening the three fires, activating the compassion fire, forming the pakuas by chanting the eight forces, forming the collection points, fusing the colors, and forming the pearl. Review the processes and explanations as needed. Once you feel the pearl is strong and full of energy, you do not have to go through all these stages every time. Just think and let it happen.

Open the Thrusting Channels in four stages: to the diaphragm; to the neck; to and out of the crown; down to the feet and into the ground, and up to the crown.

1. The Left Thrusting Channel penetrates the left testicle (in men), left side of the perineum and anus, left ovary (in women), left kidney, spleen, heart, left lung, left parathyroid and thyroid glands, left ear, left eye, and left hemisphere of the brain.
2. The Middle Thrusting Channel runs through the middle of the scrotum (in men), perineum, middle of the anus, cervix (in women), prostate (in men), aorta, vena cava, pancreas, stomach, heart, thymus gland, throat, tongue, pituitary, hypothalmus and pineal glands, and crown.
3. The Right Thrusting Channel goes through the right testicle (men), right side of the perineum and anus, right ovary (women), right kidney, liver, right lung, right parathyroid and thyroid glands, right ear, right eye, and right hemisphere of the brain.

Note: Avoid overheating the heart, liver, or head. Be very gentle with this procedure. If the energy reaches the heart and head too quickly the heart will become congested and you may experience pressure. If the heart overheats with energy, avoid thrusting above the diaphragm, and practice the heart sound (haw-w-w-w-w).

Strengthen your anal muscle, which is the foundation, connected to the perineum and everything in the body above it. Saliva purifies the mouth and nourishes immortality. When resting, create and gather saliva. Make it thick and swallow it forcefully.

Opening the Belt Channels

The Belt Channel is a psychic channel of power and self-defense that encircles the body with energy. It protects the body and fences the energy within the Governor, Functional, and Thrusting Channels, while warding off negative energy from the outside world. Starting at the navel, each chi center of the body is crossed and encircled by one level of the continuing Belt Channel. (Although the Belt Channel is really one continuous spiral, we often refer to it in the plural—the Belt Channels—in reference to these distinct levels of the channel.).

A cross-section at the navel level would show the Belt Channel connecting to the other channels you have learned to this point. At the front of the body, the Belt Channel connects with the Functional Channel. As it moves to the left side, it connects with the Left Thrusting Channel. At the Door of Life in the back, it connects with the Governor Channel. To the right, it connects with the Right Thrusting Channel. Returning to the front, the circle is completed.

When, practicing Fusion I, you learn to form a pearl and you draw the energy from the front, back, and side pakuas at the level of the navel, you are laying the groundwork for the Belt Channels.

The Belt Channel energy flow begins at the navel and spirals upward in a counterclockwise direction through the solar plexus, heart, throat, mid-eyebrow, and crown. Then you reverse the energy flow and circle the pearl clockwise as you move back down through the above points to the navel. From the navel, continue down to the sexual center, perineum, knees (around both knees), and soles of the feet (slightly into the ground). Finally, reverse the direction and work up through each point back to the navel (fig. 8.1).

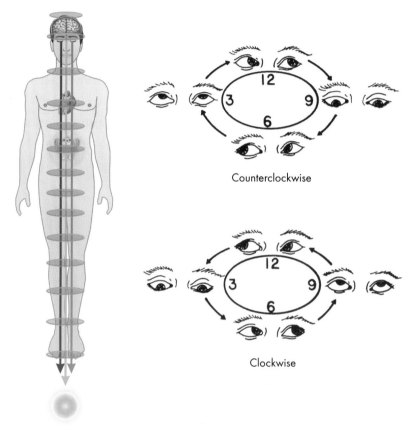

Fig. 8.1. Use the eyes to help spiral.

Note: To circle to the left is to circle counterclockwise; circle counterclockwise as you move the pearl up. To circle to the right is clockwise; circle clockwise as you move the pearl down.

The pearl is circulated in each Belt Channel 9 times. After the ninth time of circling each point, you will cross each channel internally with the pearl by moving the pearl from front to back, and from left side to right side. Each time, you will end with the pearl at the front, and then will move on to the next level of the Belt Channel.

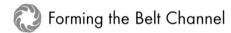
Forming the Belt Channel

Ascending from the Pakuas

1. Sit up, back straight, shoulders relaxed, feet touching the floor. Hold the hands together, and touch the tongue to the palate.
2. Practice the Inner Smile, Fusion I, chanting, forming the collection points, fusing the energy into a pearl, and the Creation Cycle of Fusion II. Continue with your practice of Cosmic Fusion by sending the energy through the three full Thrusting Channels, all the way down to the feet and up to the head (fig. 8.2).

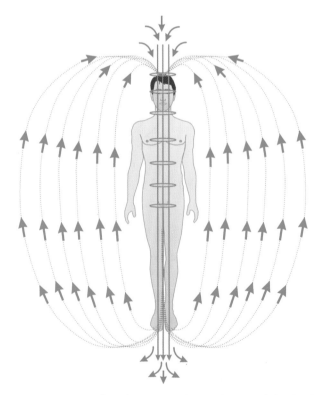

Fig. 8.2. Moving the Thrusting Channels out of the body

3. You are ready to begin forming the Belt Channel. First, form the four pakuas and a pearl. Gather the pearl at the cauldron, and bring it to the navel.

4. Join the four pakuas by circulating the pearl from the navel toward the left side (counterclockwise), to the Door of Life, to the right side, and back to the navel.

   In the beginning you can use your hand to assist you in moving the pearl, although your goal is to use your senses to control its movement. Cover the navel with the right hand. Cover the left-side pakua with the left hand. Then, move the left hand to cover the Door of Life, and move your right hand to cover the right-side pakua. Finally, return the right hand to the navel.

   Circle the pearl 9 times counterclockwise. As you are ascending you will circle it 9 times counterclockwise from each point in a similar fashion.

5. When you finish circling the pakuas for 9 rounds, be aware of the navel. Be aware of the channel of the navel. Form a cross by bringing the pearl from the navel to the cauldron, and all the way back to the Door of Life. Then, bring the pearl back to the cauldron, and use it to connect the side pakuas from the left across to the right. Return the pearl to the navel.

6. Move the pearl up from the navel to the left side of the rib cage, to a position level with the solar plexus. Begin to circle the pearl at the solar plexus level. Circle the pearl toward the left through T11 at the back, to the right, and return to the solar plexus. Circle 9 times, ending with the pearl at the solar plexus. Take a moment to perceive it. Then create an internal cross with the pearl, moving it from front to back, and then from left to right.

7. Bring the pearl from the solar plexus to the left-side rib cage, this time at the level of the heart. Circle 9 times toward the left to the middle of the shoulder blades, to the right, and back to the heart center. Circle in this manner for 9 rounds. Using the pearl, form an internal cross connecting all four sides. Feel the connection of the channel.

8. From the heart center, bring the pearl up to the left side of the throat center on the neck. Circle the pearl toward the left and back to C7, to the right side, and to the middle of the throat center, 9 times. Use the pearl to form an internal cross connecting all four sides. Practice and master this step before continuing up to the crown.

9. Bring the pearl up to the upper tip of the left ear at the level of the mid-eyebrow center (fig. 8.3). Circle the pearl 9 times from the left ear back to the small brain, to the right (upper tip of the ear), returning to the mid-eyebrow. Feel a band of energy flowing around the mid-eyebrow, ears, and back of the head. Using the pearl, form an internal cross connecting all four sides. The feeling is one of wearing a crown with a cross at its center connecting it.

10. From the mid-eyebrow bring the pearl up to the left side of the crown, and circle the energy 9 times in a counterclockwise direction at the crown. End with the pearl at the front. Using the pearl, form a cross, connecting the front, back, and both sides of this Belt Channel.

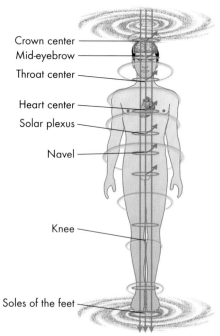

Crown center
Mid-eyebrow
Throat center

Heart center
Solar plexus

Navel

Knee

Soles of the feet

Fig. 8.3. Bring the pearl up to the upper tip of the left ear.

11. Allow the pearl to go out above the crown, and circle the energy 9 times toward the left to form a halo of energy. Use the pearl to cross the halo, front to back, and left to right. Collect the energy from above the head (fig. 8.4).

Fig. 8.4. Spiral out counterclockwise above the crown.

12. Now reverse the direction of energy flow to a clockwise direction by circling from the front toward the right, to the back, and to the left (see fig. 8.5 on the following page). Circle the halo 9 times, ending with the pearl at the front. Then cross the front to back, and right to left sides. Finish by bringing the pearl to the front of the halo.

13. Next, bring the pearl back into the right side of the crown. Circle toward the right 9 times, bringing the pearl to the back, to the left, and ending at the front of the crown each time. Then use the pearl to cross the front, back, and two sides. Return the pearl to the front of the crown.

14. Move the pearl down to the upper tip of the right ear. Circle from the right ear to the back of the head, to the top of the left ear, and

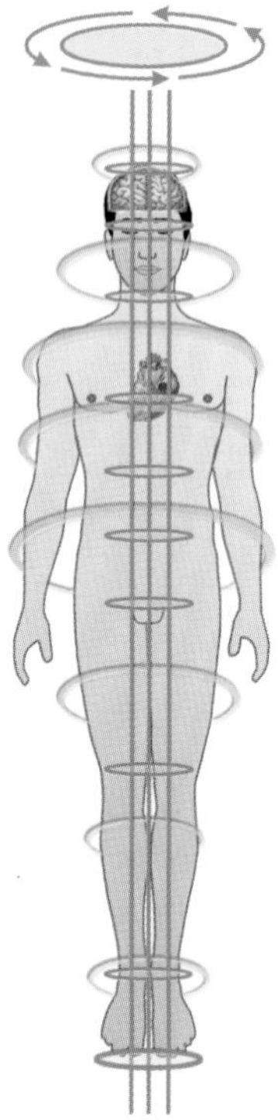

Fig. 8.5. Reverse
the direction
clockwise.

to the mid-eyebrow 9 times. End at the mid-eyebrow. Use the
pearl to cross the front, back, and two sides at this level, and return
it to the front to the mid-eyebrow position.

15. Bring the pearl down to the right side of the neck at the level of
the throat center, and circle right to C7 at the back of the neck, to
the left, and to the front of the throat center. Circle 9 times, ending at the front. Cross the front, back, and two sides, also ending
by bringing the pearl to the front.

16. Bring the pearl down to the right-side rib cage at the heart center
level. Circle the pearl toward the right, to the back, and so forth
clockwise for 9 times, ending at the front of the heart center.
Then, use the pearl to cross the front, back, and two sides. Return
the pearl to the front again.

17. Move the pearl to the solar plexus. Circle it 9 times to T11 at the
back, and return it to the solar plexus. Cross the front, back, and
sides. Return the pearl to the front.

18. Bring the pearl down to the navel. Circle it back to the Door of Life, and back to the navel, 9 times. From the navel bring the pearl to the cauldron, back toward the Door of Life, and return it to the cauldron. Use the pearl to cross the right and left sides. Return the pearl to the navel.

❂ Descending from the Pakuas to the Earth

1. Once you have controlled the pearl to this stage of the meditation, you are ready to move the pearl down to the sexual center. Women bring the pearl down to the right side of the Ovary Palace, located 3 inches below the navel. Men bring the pearl from the navel down to the right side of the Sperm Palace, $1^{1}/_{2}$ inches below the navel. Circle clockwise back to the sacrum, to the left hip, and to the front of the Ovary Palace/Sperm Palace 9 times. Use the pearl to make a cross. Return the pearl to the front of the sexual center.

2. Bring the pearl down to the right groin. Circle the pearl clockwise around the perineum point and lower hips 9 times. Use the pearl to form a cross by connecting the front, back, and sides. Return the pearl to the front.

3. Move the energy down and circle toward the back of both knees, around and to the front, midway between both knees, moving the pearl clockwise 9 times. Use the pearl to form a cross by moving the pearl to the midpoint between the knees and connecting the front, back, and sides from this point. End with the pearl midway between the fronts of both knees.

4. Direct the energy down to the feet, just below the ankles. Circle the soles of the feet 9 times, moving the pearl clockwise to the heel of the right foot, to the heel of the left foot, to the outer side of the left foot, to the front, midway between both feet. Form a cross. End with the pearl midway between both feet.

5. Move the energy from the front of the feet down to a point beneath the earth, and circle toward the right (clockwise) 9 times

(fig. 8.6). Use the pearl to form a cross beneath the earth. Keep on spiraling more energy to enhance the pearl. Return the pearl to the front of the circle.

Ascending From the Earth Back to the Pakuas

1. Reverse the circle beneath the earth, moving the pearl counterclockwise again 9 times (fig. 8.7). Use the pearl to form a cross, connecting the front, back, and sides.
2. Move the pearl to the outer side of the left foot. Circle the soles of both feet 9 times, moving toward the left heel, to the right heel, to the right foot, and to the front (midway) of both feet. Use the pearl to form a cross. End with the pearl at the midway point in the front of both feet.

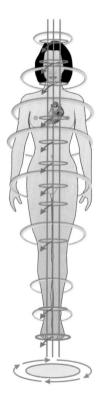
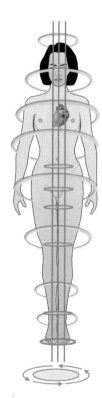

Fig. 8.6. Bring the pearl down to the ground, spiraling counterclockwise.

Fig. 8.7. Spiral reverse clockwise moving up.

3. Move up to the left knee. Circle the pearl counterclockwise at the knees 9 times. Use the pearl to form a cross. Return the pearl to the midway point in the front of both knees.

4. From the front of the knees, move up to the left groin area. Circle counterclockwise at the perineum 9 times. Use the pearl to form a cross. Return the pearl to the front of the perineum.

5. Direct the energy to the left hip, and circle counterclockwise at the Ovary Palace/Sperm Palace 9 times. Use the pearl to form a cross by connecting the front, back, and sides. End with the pearl at the front of the Ovary Palace/Sperm Palace.

6. Return the pearl to the navel and to the cauldron (fig. 8.8).

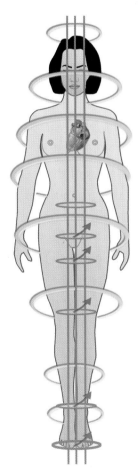

Fig. 8.8. Bring the pearl up to the navel.

Men and Women Practice Differently

Men: Shoot the Pearl Out of the Crown, and Spiral the Pearl Down

1. Bring the pearl up to the crown.
2. Allow the pearl to go out 3 to 6 inches above the head. Circle 9 times counterclockwise. Collect the heavenly energy and blend it in the pearl. Then circle it 9 times clockwise.
3. Bring the pearl back into the crown point.
4. Spiral it clockwise through each of the Belt Channels all the way down to the soles of the feet.
5. Move the pearl into the earth 6 to 12 inches to collect the earth energy, and circle the energy 9 times clockwise. Reverse the direction, spiraling 9 times counterclockwise.
6. Return the pearl to the front of the crown, and then back down to the navel and cauldron in the same manner.

Women: Shoot the Pearl into the Earth, and Spiral the Pearl Up from the Earth

1. Bring the pearl to the soles of the feet.
2. Move the pearl into the ground 6 to 12 inches to collect the earthly energy. Circle the energy 9 times clockwise. Then circle it 9 times counterclockwise.
3. Move the pearl up through the left side of each Belt Channel, spiraling counterclockwise to the crown.
4. Shoot the pearl all the way out at the crown to collect the heavenly energy. Circle the energy counterclockwise 9 times. Reverse the direction, and spiral the pearl 9 times clockwise.
5. Bring the pearl back down into the right side of the crown. Continue to spiral the energy clockwise down through the Belt Channel to the soles of the feet. Return the pearl to the navel and cauldron in the same manner.

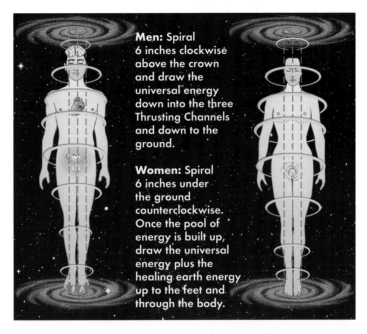

Men: Spiral 6 inches clockwise above the crown and draw the universal energy down into the three Thrusting Channels and down to the ground.

Women: Spiral 6 inches under the ground counterclockwise. Once the pool of energy is built up, draw the universal energy plus the healing earth energy up to the feet and through the body.

Fig. 8.9. Men and women practice differently.

🌀 Forming a Vehicle

Continue feeling all the pakuas spiraling around the energy center and around the body (fig. 8.10).

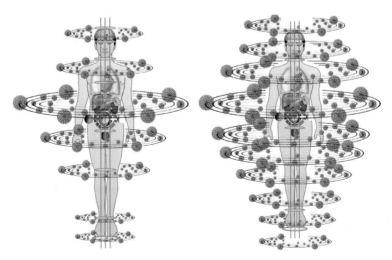

Fig. 8.10. Spiraling the pearl and pakuas faster and faster

Let the pakuas spiral faster; start from 10,000 miles per hour and work up to 60,000 miles per hour, and feel the spine getting bigger and bigger (fig. 8.11).

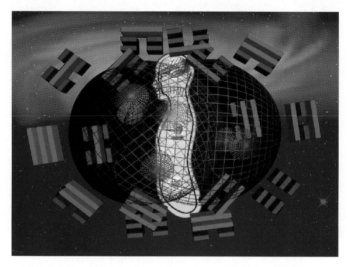

Fig. 8.11. All the pakuas become a bigger and bigger pakua spiraling around the whole body.

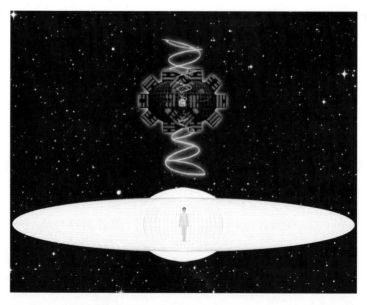

Fig. 8.12. The spirals of the pakua become a very large pakua and form a spaceship up to 50 meters in diameter or larger.

Summary: Procedure of Forming the Belt Channels

Ascending from the Pakuas

1. Practice the Inner Smile, form the compassion fire, chant the pakuas, form the collection points, fuse the energy into a pearl, and practice the Creation Cycle of Fusion II.

2. Send energy through the three Thrusting Channels all the way down to the feet and up to the head.

3. Form the four pakuas and a pearl. Gather the pearl at the cauldron, and bring it to the navel.

4. Join the four pakuas by circulating the pearl from the navel counterclockwise to the Door of Life and back to the navel. Continue circling the pearl 9 times around the Thrusting Channels and around the body counterclockwise.

5. Form a cross. Bring the pearl from the navel to the cauldron, and back to the Door of Life. Use it to connect the side pakuas. Return the pearl to the navel.

6. From navel move to the left side of the solar plexus. Begin to circle the pearl at the solar plexus level. Circle the pearl to the left through T11 and return to the solar plexus. Circle 9 times. Create an internal cross with the pearl.

7. Bring the pearl to the left side of the heart. Circle 9 times toward the left, to the middle of the shoulder blades, and back to the heart center. Use the pearl to form an internal cross connecting all four sides.

8. Next bring the pearl to the left side of the throat center. Circle the pearl back to C7, and to the middle of the throat center, 9 times. Form an internal cross. Practice and master this step before continuing up to the crown.

9. Bring the pearl to the upper tip of the left ear level with the mid-eyebrow. Circle the pearl 9 times back to the small brain, to the upper tip of the right ear, returning to the mid-eyebrow. Feel a band of energy flowing around the mid-eyebrow, ears, and back of the head. Form an internal cross connecting all four sides.

10. Bring the pearl to the left side of the crown. Circle the energy 9 times counterclockwise at the crown. Connect the front, back, and both sides of this Belt Channel.

11. Allow the pearl out above the crown. Circle the energy 9 times forming a halo of energy. Use the pearl to cross the halo, front to back, and left to right. Collect the energy from above the head.

Descending Back to the Pakuas

12. Reverse the energy flow to a clockwise direction. Circle the halo 9 times. Then cross it front to back, and right to left sides.

13. Bring the pearl back to the crown. Circle to the right 9 times. Then use the pearl to cross the front, back, and two sides.

14. Move the pearl down to the upper tip of the right ear. Circle from the right ear to the mid-eyebrow. Repeat 9 times. Use the pearl to form a cross and return it to mid-eyebrow.

15. Bring the pearl down to the right side of the neck at the throat center. Circle right to C7 at the back of the neck. Return to the front again. Circle 9 times. Cross the front, back, and two sides. Bring the pearl to the front.

16. Bring the pearl down to the right side of the heart center. Circle it clockwise 9 times, ending at the front. Then, use the pearl to cross the front, back, and sides. Return the pearl to the front again.

17. Move the pearl to the solar plexus. Circle it 9 times to T11 at the back, and return to the solar plexus. Cross the front, back, and sides. Return the pearl to the front.

18. Bring the pearl down to the navel. Circle it back to the Door of Life, and back to the navel 9 times. From the navel bring the pearl to the cauldron, back toward the Door of Life, and return it to the cauldron. Use the pearl to cross the right and left sides. Return the pearl to the navel.

Descending from the Pakuas to the Earth

19. Once you have controlled the pearl to this stage of the meditation, you are ready to move the pearl down to the sexual center. Women bring the pearl down to the right side of the ovary center, located 3 inches below the navel. Men bring the pearl from the navel down to the right side of the sperm palace, $1^1/_2$ inches below the navel. Circle clockwise back to the sacrum, to the left hip, and to the front of the ovary center/sperm palace 9 times. Use the pearl to make a cross. Return the pearl to the front of the sexual center.

20. Bring the pearl down to the right groin. Circle the pearl clockwise around the perineum point and lower hips 9 times. Use the pearl to form a cross by connecting the front, back, and sides. Return the pearl to the front.

21. Move the energy down and circle toward the back of both knees, around and to the front, midway between both knees, moving the pearl clockwise 9 times. Use the pearl to form a cross by moving the pearl to the midpoint between the knees and connecting the front, back, and sides from this point. End with the pearl midway between the fronts of both knees.

22. Direct the energy down to the feet, just below the ankles. Circle the soles of the feet 9 times, moving the pearl clockwise to the heel of the right foot, to the heel of the left foot, to the outer side of the left foot, to the front, midway between both feet. Form a cross. End with the pearl midway between both feet.

23. Move the energy from the front of the feet down to a point beneath the earth, and circle toward the right (clockwise) 9 times. Use the pearl to form a cross beneath the earth. Keep on spiraling more energy to enhance the pearl. Return the pearl to the front of the circle.

24. Reverse the circle beneath the earth, moving the pearl counterclockwise again 9 times. Use the pearl to form a cross, connecting the front, back, and sides.
25. Move the pearl to the outer side of the left foot. Circle the soles of both feet 9 times moving toward the left heel, to the right heel, to the right foot, and to the front (midway) of both feet. Use the pearl to form a cross. End with the pearl at the midway point in the front of both feet.
26. Move up to the left knee. Circle the pearl counterclockwise at the knees 9 times. Use the pearl to form a cross. Return the pearl to the midway point in the front of both knees.
27. From the front of the knees, move up to the left groin area. Circle counterclockwise at the perineum 9 times. Use the pearl to form a cross. Return the pearl to the front of the perineum.
28. Direct the energy to the left hip, and circle counterclockwise at the Ovary Palace/Sperm Palace 9 times. Use the pearl to form a cross by connecting the front, back, and sides. End with the pearl at the front of the Ovary Palace/Sperm Palace.
29. Return the pearl to the navel and to the cauldron.

Men and Women Practice Differently

See the section earlier in the chapter that describes in detail how men and women practice from this point on.

THE ENERGY BODY

Once you have practiced to this level, you are ready to form the pearl into the energy body or soul body (fig. 8.13).

Sorcerers saw that the essence of the universe resembled a matrix of energy shot through by incandescent strands of consciousness or actual awareness. They also "saw" the essence of the human form. It was not merely an apelike amalgamation of skin and bones, but an

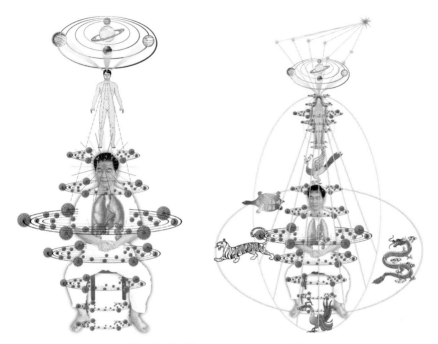

Fig. 8.13. The energy or soul body

egg-shaped ball of luminosity capable of traveling along those incandescent strands to other worlds.*

Just as it is important for the physical body to be strong so we can enjoy optimum health, it is also vital to strengthen the soul body so it becomes a sturdy vehicle for our consciousness. Strengthening chi nourishes our health and spiritual qualities in this life and builds a strong soul body to carry us forth into the "afterlife" (which is, paradoxically, the here and now). We begin to strengthen the soul body through what is called, in Taoist Internal Alchemy, the Inner Elixir. It is called the Inner Elixir because we are working with the energies already within our own body and converting them into elixir-like healing essences. Through the meditation practices of the Microcosmic Orbit and the Fusion of the Five Elements, we detoxify, nourish, and integrate the physical body, the energy body, and the emotions.

---

*See the article by Bruce Wagner, "You Only Live Twice," in *Details*, March 1994, 168.

Forming the Pearl into the Soul Body

1. Always begin by doing the Fusion I practice to clean out the negative emotions.
2. Chant the eight forces and form the collection points. Let the pakua spin around the physical body.
3. Condense the pearl and practice the Creation Cycle, Thrusting Channels, and Belt Channels.
4. Run the pearl in the Microcosmic Orbit, and control its movement with the senses.
5. Move the pearl to the perineum. Inhale in short sips, drawing in 10 percent of the lungs' capacity, while gently pulling up the anus. Inhale up to the navel, then to the heart.
6. Inhale up to the crown. Swallow your saliva (imagine swallowing upward) and exhale forcefully to open the crown and shoot the pearl out.
7. Practice moving the pearl up to 1 foot, then 2 feet, then 3, 4, 5, and 6 feet above your head. Go out only as far as you are able to maintain control of the pearl.
8. Relax the senses, and form the soul body.
9. Run the pearl in the Microcosmic Orbit in the physical body. Open the crown, transfer the Microcosmic pathway into the soul body above the head.
10. Form another pearl in the cauldron, and shoot the pearl into the soul body.
11. Circulate the pearl through the Microcosmic Orbits in both the physical and energy bodies together.
12. Extend the Thrusting Channels up into the soul body.
13. Practice all the Belt Channels up through the head, or down through the soles, into the soul body. Spiral all the pakuas around the soul body like a spaceship.
14. Continue to practice until you are in full control of the soul body.

Note: You can also form a soul body below you by thrusting the pearl through the soles of the feet into the ground.

THE SPIRIT BODY

Once you are well in control of the soul body, you are ready to form the spirit body (fig. 8.14).

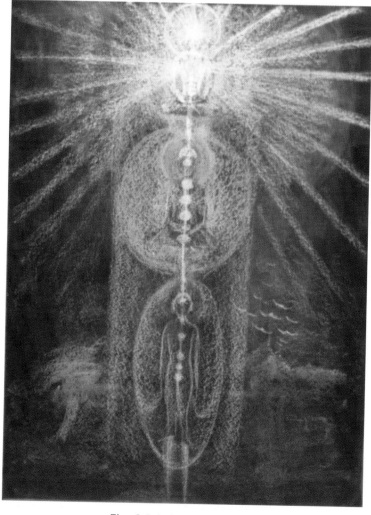

Fig. 8.14. Spiritual being

Forming the Spirit Body

Stage One

Be aware of the four pakuas in each center and spiral them around the physical body and the energy body.

1. Begin to form the spirit body after doing the soul body practice. Leave the soul body above the crown. Form another pearl at the cauldron, and run the Creation Cycle.
2. Form the pearl from compassion energy, a pearl that is more blue and gold than the soul body pearl.
3. Move this pearl in the Microcosmic Orbit. Bring it down to the perineum.
4. Inhale in small sips, and pull up the anus. Inhale the pearl to the navel; then to the heart, and then to the crown.
5. Inhale again, and swallow up. Exhale forcefully to open the crown, and project the pearl to the perineum of the energy body.
6. Exhale, and send the pearl to the heart of the soul body. Exhale again, and send the pearl above the crown of the soul body.
7. Move the pearl up and down approximately 12 inches (30 centimeters) above the crown of the soul body. Then gradually extend the pearl further up in 1 foot (30 centimeters) increments. Practice until you are able to move the pearl up and down 6 feet above the energy body.
8. Condense the pearl. Condense the soul body. Bring both pearls back to the cauldron of the physical body.

Stage Two

1. Repeat steps 1 to 7 above, and run the Microcosmic Orbit in the physical and energy bodies.
2. Transfer the Microcosmic Orbit from the soul body into the spirit body, and then run the three Microcosmic Orbits together. As an alternative, you can run the Microcosmic Orbit as one large channel incorporating all three bodies.

3. Extend the Thrusting Channels to the spirit body.

4. Extend the Belt Channels to the spirit body.

5. Finish by condensing the energy of both the soul and spirit bodies into a pearl. Pull the pearl into the physical body.

6. Collect the energy at the cauldron, and practice Chi Massage.

Fusion as a Bridge

Joost Kuitenbrouwer, Universal Tao Instructor

In the overall structure of the Universal Tao, the Fusion practices serve as a bridge between the basic preparatory practices—such as the Inner Smile, the Healing Sounds, the Microcosmic Orbit, Healing Love, Tao Yin, Iron Shirt Chi Kung, Cosmic Chi Kung, Bone Marrow Nei Kung, and Tai Chi—and the higher Internal Alchemy practices of Kan and Li.

The Fusion practices are traditionally considered to be the beginnings of Internal Alchemy, as they focus on the transformation of the emotional energies contained in the major organs of the body. The organs are, in turn, considered to be centers and fields of energy that resonate, each with their particular frequencies, with the energies and forces of the universe.

The body gradually becomes more open through a process of balancing negative and positive energies (Fusion of the Five Elements), the growth of positive energies (Cosmic Fusion), and the opening of meridians to enhance the circulation of internal energies of the body and to make it receptive for outside energies (Fusion of the Psychic Channels). Thereby the self-healing process, initiated in the basic practices, is further enhanced.

Once the body's strength and health have been increased, so that it can serve as a vessel for the forces of the universe and is in a position to process them, it is ready for the higher alchemy of the Kan and Li practices, in which the physical body can give birth to the energy body, and that body can birth the spirit body, also called the light or rainbow body.

FUSION AS A JOURNEY OF SELF-TRANSFORMATION

In the Fusion practices, first the body and its path routes are cleansed and opened, so that the energy from within and from without can flow with more power and ease. Then, the energy flows in the body are qualitatively raised, further enhancing the self-healing and regenerative capacity of the body, already initiated in the basic practices. As a result, the body's health and vitality receive a new boost and it grows in strength. At the same time, it becomes more able to absorb and process the various forces and energies from the universe, the cosmos, and nature.

In the Fusion practices, the body enters into a dynamic process toward new balances. This is an essential condition for the light to grow inside. This light can then in turn attract the light from heaven as its energies become finer, as they blend into a higher quality of energy created by the blending of love and compassion. This higher concentration of energy is then condensed into a pearl and circulated through the major organs and the psychic channels in and around the body. The pearl helps the body to feel centered and to experience peace and harmony. It also helps to cleanse the special channels and enhance the free flow of energy.

The pearl will facilitate the growth and transference of consciousness from the physical to the energy body and from the energy to the spirit body (Cosmic Fusion), healing it and helping it to center and experience peace and harmony. Through the growth of love and compassion the body is able to radiate out, and receive in, the love and cosmic energies, so that its own chi is blended with the cosmic chi and is thereby transformed into a higher quality of chi.

To facilitate the blending and balancing of energies between the organs of the body, and the gathering, processing, and condensing of energies from the universe and from nature, the pakuas play an essential role (Formula 1, Fusion of the Five Elements).

In the earliest stage after conception, when the body is forming, the Governor and Conception Channels are the first meridians to rule the circulation of energy in the embryo. Successively, all other yin and yang meridians form in a symmetric fashion on the yang and yin sides of the body. In ancient Taoists texts, these are also called the sun side or outer side, and the moon side or inner side of the body. The sun side is that side exposed to the sun when one bows down; the moon side is the part that remains in the shadow.

We might visualize the body as a grid of conduits of light that link it to the Light, in which all energy and matter have their origin. This view is supported by the new physics.

THE UNITY OF YING AND YANG

Basic to the Taoist tradition is the view that positive and negative energies are a manifestation of the very nature of the universe as a unity of opposite energies: the yin and the yang. It is by virtue of the dynamics of the interplay of yin and yang that the universe comes into existence and continues to exist. These opposite energies rule all phenomena in the universe as an infinite web of mutually interconnected processes and their movement. This insight is the theoretical as well as the practical basis of the Fusion practices.

In Taoist theory, yin and yang rule the relationships between stars, planets, the sun and the moon and the earth, light and dark, above and below, man and woman. It is in and through this interplay that the universe unfolds and functions. If one of them disintegrated or disappeared, the universe would end.

In the Taoist vision of the nature of the universe, the body is a microcosm that manifests and reflects in its inner structure the dynamics of the universe. As such, it is also ruled by the same forces of yin and yang.

These forces in turn manifest themselves in the universe in the five elements—water, fire, wood, metal, and earth. These five elements operate as energies in the body, in and through the five major organs: the kidney, heart, liver, lungs, and spleen. It is the natural capacity of the body to heal and regenerate itself. The body is sustained and nurtured by cooperating with and facilitating the workings of the universe, through balancing the five forces in the organs of the body and the positive and negative properties of each of them. The relationship between the positive and negative energies contained and reflected in the organs is the starting point of the Fusion practices.

In the Taoist tradition, the body has always been viewed as a sacred vessel, reflecting the sacred nature of the universe as a whole. When the laws of motion are interfered with, the balance between yin and yang is lost, and with it, the harmony and cooperation between the organs and the elements that compose the body. As a result, the free flow of energy streams is inhibited, and the immunity of the body is affected. Chinese medicine, of Taoist origin, sees disease as the outward manifestation of imbalances within the body. Hence the predominant attention in Chinese medicine and Taoist self-healing practice on the balancing and strengthening of the organs and their cooperative relationships.

The Taoist view on the outer and inner universe (the body) is the fruit of several thousand years of highly sophisticated empirical observation. A resulting insight is that the use of feelings and sensations in the body plays a crucial role in creating balance within the body and its processes and needs, and between its organs and their energies, so that inner peace and harmony may grow (Formula 2, Fusion of the Five Elements).

TURNING INWARD

Such growth involves a process of turning inward and to feel and sense oneself "from within" so that understanding can grow. This in turn further supports the effectiveness of the inward-oriented process of listening. By turning the senses inward and reconnecting them with their corresponding organs (ears/kidneys, eyes/liver, tongue/heart,

mouth/spleen, nose/lungs), the process of externalizing the consciousness and thereby draining the energies out of the body can be inverted.
This allows the body to come to rest and recuperate its energies and
the connected senses.

When we protect the senses from undue outside influences, the
life force energies in the body and the higher energies it accumulates
are preserved and can grow without interference. This accumulation
occurs through the blending of energies from all the directions, but
especially those from the stars and the sun and moon and planets (Formula 3, Cosmic Fusion). This process of protection is further deep-
ened and completed in the high formula of Sealing the Five Senses, in
the Kan and Li practices, when we create protective auras around the
body from the accumulated energies of each of the major organs.

There is abundant evidence that, in the externalization imposed on
the body in the process of modernization and its growing pressures,
the senses have become atrophied. By turning the senses inward, it
becomes easier to control them and protect the integrity of the body
and its organs so that it can regenerate.

The Taoist approach to the body is rooted in the vision that there
is an inner order in the very nature of the universe and all its manifestations. The outer order is a manifestation and reflection of this
inner order. If the outer order is in harmony with the inner order, then
harmony and peace reign.

As our receptivity and ability to sense and feel ourselves from
within grows, so grows our ability to experience the universe within
ourselves. By looking deeply into ourselves we grow. Our understanding of our being and body as a microcosm, and its intrinsic unity with
the universe as a macrocosm, grows.

FROM BALANCE, THROUGH
RESONANCE, TO LOVE

As we ourselves, and our body and its chemistry, are changing, our consciousness and perceptions also change and widen. A point will come

where we begin to experience ourselves less as separate and isolated from the universe and more in resonance and in tune with the universe.

In this process, we grow more aware of the wavelike nature of our body in and through which the universe pulses, and how we pulse in and through our bodies with the energies and forces of the universe. At the same time, our ability to tune in with the energy of the universe and its frequencies and to absorb and draw this energy into ourselves will grow.

The Fusion practices serve an essential function in making our being more open through the heightened sensitivity of the body, as our energies become purified and more fine and subtle. The desire rises within the body to enter into the primordial unity with the original energy, its causal source as a living being.

In the ancient Taoist vision, this relationship has always been seen as a love relationship that reveals itself when our body returns to its inner balance, and yin and yang enter into balance. The ability to attract and conduct the energies from the universe into a body through the network of conduits, represented by the grid of meridians, depends on the quality of the inner work toward unity between yin and yang.

This meeting between yin and yang has in the Taoist tradition been seen as a marriage, born out of love between the opposites, as they move toward unity. The Fusion practices play an important role in the preparation of a state of being that makes this movement toward unity possible.

ENLIGHTENMENT OF THE BODY AND THE NEW PHYSICS

The Taoist insight—that human beings, with all other phenomena, have common origins in the universe and that those origins are in the stars and the heavens—is shared in many other ancient cosmologies: those of the African peoples, the indigenous peoples of North and South America, and the Australian aboriginal people.

The Taoist tradition, however, is unique in that, over time, it has evolved concrete practical formulas and practices to work with. These help us to reconnect and, in the process, rediscover the inherent ecstatic nature of our body, through the process of self-transformation.

These formulas, of which the Fusion practices are an integral part, are based on the insight into the nature of the meridians and their application in healing the body and restoring its natural functions, the goal of Chinese medicine.

Another closely related Taoist tenet on the nature of the universe, also found in all ancient cosmological traditions (including those of the West, before the scientific revolution did away with them, viewing them as superstition), is the unity, indivisibility, and interchangeability of matter and energy.

This concept finds full support in the new physics, which evolved from the beginning of the twentieth century with the path-breaking discoveries in quantum physics and relativity theory by the great physicists Bohr, Einstein, and Heisenberg. Their discoveries shattered the foundations of the old paradigm, the Cartesian-Newtonian physics underlying the basis of modern science. They broke radically new ground in the interpretation of the nature of matter. In the new vision of advanced physics, matter is understood as a process and an event. Matter and energy are forms of the same reality. As matter can change into energy, energy can also change into matter. Both matter and energy are viewed in this new interpretation of reality as having their origin in light.

Therefore, the Taoist vision on the intrinsic nature of the body as a *light body* is not a romantic vision, invented by creative minds. The image corresponds to the insights of advanced physics. Thus what has been called in ancient spiritual traditions "enlightenment" refers to a real material process: the illumination of the body.

Here is what distinguishes the Taoist vision from most others: enlightenment is understood not as a process that happens "in the mind," separate from the body; rather, the process takes place in and through the body and its progressive transformation.

Thus, a true process of spiritual growth in the Taoist vision implies the enlightenment of the body. The progressive process of illumination is a bodily process, visible to the eye and tangible in the quality of energy that a person manifests and radiates in her/his body. This emphasis on transformation as a bodily process is a principal characteristic of the Taoist tradition. In this respect it differs from other systems marked by the duality of body and mind and in which the body is viewed as a stumbling block, a hindrance.

This also explains the Taoist insistence on the central importance of rooting and grounding the body in the process of self-transformation. The more we advance in the higher practices, the greater the need to root and ground so that the energies in the body remain in balance. Equally important is centering, through which we maintain and enhance the balance between heaven and earth, the energies from above and below.

It is precisely for this reason Taoist practice gives the highest priority to the creation of a healthy and strong body, through a healthy and relaxed lifestyle and an intelligent natural diet—thanks to which the body can continuously regenerate and rejuvenate itself.

These insights are congruent with the new view of the nature of electromagnetic waves as particular forms of energy, and with the view that light is an electromagnetic field taking the form of waves that can travel through empty space (also called ether) as very light vibrations. Both the Chinese and Indian cosmologies see this energy as the mother energy from which the other elements originate and which compose the universe, the cosmos, and nature: wood and fire, earth and metal and water.

In the Taoist system, these elements correspond to the seasons, temperatures, senses, colors, sounds, and positive and negative emotions. They form the theoretical and practical starting point for the Fusion practices.

A RETURN TO COSMOLOGY

The revolutionary implications for our perceptions of the universe, the cosmos, time and space, and of nature and ourselves as part of nature, are only slowly penetrating into the social consciousness. The conditioning and fixations in major cultural patterns, and corresponding perceptions of reality, prevent the social consciousness from being open to an understanding of our true nature.

Multiple mechanics at work in present-day culture and science keep us attached to the current mindset. This mindset is rooted in the subconscious, which rules the conscious mind, unaware of the forces by which it is steered. In this mindset, it appears as if the universe is composed of an infinite amount of loosely, accidentally assembled particles and solid objects, each having an independent, separate existence, rather than what is actually an ever unceasingly changing web of events, all mutually interconnected and interdependent.

What has emerged in Western history and culture is the idea of human beings as essentially sovereign and independent from the universe, and the rulers of the universe, who can alter life and the origins of life at will, through the progress of science and technology. The Taoist vision wholly questions this belief.

Mirroring the basic premises of the Cartesian-Newtonian paradigm, this presumed independence and freedom from the laws of motion of the universe has also shaped the basic assumptions about the nature of human beings and social relations, which in turn have shaped mainstream social science and psychology. These support a view of progress and development, the new version of which emerged in the course of the twentieth century, essentially inspired by the notion that reality can be manipulated and engineered without regard for the consequences on Nature. However, with the more recent evidence of the adverse effects of such an attitude, and the growing concern that the very foundations supporting life on Earth are in jeopardy, many humans are questioning the basic premises of this attitude.

A natural consequence of this has been a growing interest in the visions that inspired the ancient cosmologies such as the Taoist one, especially with the increasing evidence in advanced physics to support such visions. Thus it is not surprising that a leading philosopher of science, Stephen Toulmin, recently published a book entitled *The*

*Return to Cosmology.** In his study, he traces the process of alienation in Western culture and science, as it came to shape modern life. He especially focuses on the relation between body and mind. He foresees a return to ways of looking at reality that help overcome the duality at the root of this alienation and the imbalances it has brought about in the present-day world system, and which it feeds through the new communication technologies.

At the base of Eastern epistemologies—not only basic to Taoism but also at the root of other Eastern religious and spiritual traditions—is this: that true knowledge can only be acquired experientially and existentially, in and through the *practice*. It cannot be emphasized enough that when the Universal Tao system is described as a whole of interrelated practices, it is based on this root assumption, that only in the *practice* is experience gained. The practice sets in motion a process of self-transformation that allows the practitioner to come to terms with the patterns within the self that prohibit discovering its relevance.

Also implicit in the Taoist vision, and shared in other ancient cosmologies, is the perception that the universe is alive. Not only as it births life at every instant, but also as it sustains and nurtures life. This view is quite contrary to that underlying the materialist world view, which originated with the advent of modern science, in which the universe is reduced to an accidental, anomalous phenomenon.

THE RELIGIOUS NATURE OF TAOIST PRACTICE

In the Taoist view, supported by the new physics, the body is not only matter but also a field of consciousness that, by its wavelike nature, is intrinsically related to the whole universe and can also get in touch with it. This view provides the very basis for the Cosmic Chi Kung practice, which helps to enhance and balance the body, and which is essential to the Fusion practices.

---

*Stephen Toulmin, *The Return to Cosmology: Postmodern Science and the Theology of Nature* (Berkeley: University of California Press, 1985).

Also central to the Taoist tradition is religious *practice:* emphasis is on the feeling and experiencing of the sacred and the divine, and not on the reciting of beliefs about them. Universal Tao offers a synthesis of the ancient practices, which until recently were scattered and inaccessible, except for highly fragmented information. They are being published for the first time in the West.

The Taoist view on the nature of religiosity as an experience of connection and reconnection is very much in line with the original meaning of the Latin root of the word *religion,* "re-ligare," meaning "to reconnect." Thus, the practice is oriented toward rediscovering the intrinsically ecstatic nature of the body, which spontaneously feels the truthfulness of life as a sacred, naturally ecstatic activity. The whole practice may be summarized as facilitating the process of reconnecting and returning to the state we were in before being born.

Basic to the transformation process that leads to this rediscovery is the Healing Love practice, by which the sexual energy is retained, its flow is inverted, and the nature of the energy is transformed. The Fusion practices play an essential role in making possible the further refinement of this energy in the Kan and Li practices through new forms of purification, and by enhancing the receptivity of the body for higher energies from the universe. The Taoist practice takes literally the Christian tenet that the body is the temple of God by viewing the vital energy, or life force energy, as a sacred energy through which the body reveals its divine nature as an intrinsic endowment in which heaven and earth merge.

THE WISDOM OF MAKING FRIENDS WITH THE DEVIL

The three monotheistic religious mainstreams in their institutionalized, exoteric forms—the Jewish, Christian, and Islamic—are marked by a deep duality, a schism between high and low, sacred and profane, right and wrong, good and evil, mind and matter, mind and body, mind and energy. This duality has also affected the social and institutional evolution of other religious and philosophical systems, systems such as Hinduism, Buddhism, Taoism, and Confucianism. Dualistic beliefs and codes of ethics have tended to split humankind between believers and nonbelievers and between those who are good and those who are bad.

The focus on the duality between heaven and Earth, God and the devil, good and evil, mind/spirit and body, and on sin with its corollaries of fear and guilt, has created much violence and continues to do so. That focus has also greatly affected people's sense of dignity, self-esteem, and independence, as it tends to create major dependencies on institutional intermediation with the divine.

A leading philosopher of culture and a humanist therapist in the West, Erich Fromm, has said that the propagation of these dualistic views, often accomplished in extremely violent ways, has broken the spiritual backbone of the people.

Exoteric systems have, however, never succeeded in wholly eradicating and repressing their esoteric roots, visible in movements throughout history, in which the body was considered sacred and a temple of the divine, and in which sexuality was viewed as intrinsically sacred.

In many pre-industrial cultures, proverbs and legends suggest

Fig. 9.1. The balance of yang and yin (good and bad)

that it is wise to make friends with the devil rather than fight him. It would seem that such intuitions are based on the insight that it is better to reconcile and accept oneself so that the negative loses its power, rather than opposing it, whereby its power increases. This is especially true when fear and anger rise and the negative is turned into an obsession. Simple observation confirms the truth of this insight: that the energy of what we view as negative and dark increases to the extent that there is an attempt to eradicate it. This same principle shows up in the martial arts: never initiate the fight; but let the enemy come, and neutralize him by making use of his own energy, as in Tai Chi and Aikido.

It may be said that all esoteric systems, in their origins, have called on humankind to practice love and compassion and thereby to transcend ego and enter into a state of grace. Adepts like the Jewish spiritual master Jesus, who inspired the Christian tradition, Mohammed in the Islamic tradition, and the Gautama in the Buddhist tradition, may all be seen as great masters. They showed people ways of self-transformation through the practice of love and compassion. By assuming responsibility for themselves, they could attain inner freedom and bliss and transcend themselves.

In the Taoist view, the problem with any religion or philosophy is not in its practice, but in the beliefs that serve to divide rather than unite, inside the person and outside.

THE UNITY OF LIGHT AND DARK

In the Taoist perspective, there is no sin, as light and dark are two poles of the same indivisible reality. Thus, attempts to eradicate the dark, so that light will prevail, are bound to fail and tend to lead to conflict and violence. Attempts to conquer evil at the expense of good (for example, the Crusades) are bound to generate more violence. And battles to secure good over evil will create more problems than they solve. In the Taoist view there should be neither winners nor losers (fig. 9.1).

Thus, balance between opposite forces and energies, as expres-

Fig. 9.2. The light and dark of the Tai Chi symbol are connected.

sions of yin and yang, the positive and the negative, is essential to Taoist perspective, as expressed in the Tao Te Ching, attributed to the great Taoist Master of self-transformation, Lao Tzu (fig. 9.2).

From a Taoist perspective, you enhance that balance by entering into alignment with the universe, when you actualize the universe within yourself and so are empowered and realize yourself. This state has also been called a state of selfhood, as you have returned to your original self. This process is also called "returning to your origins." This means that you have overcome the contradictions and imbalances in yourself, so that yin and yang enter into balance and harmonize. The Taoist texts speak of becoming the "Undivided Being." Lao Tzu uses the metaphor of the unhewn log (p'u). It manifests a return to the original state of spontaneity, in the old Taoist texts called "Tzu-jan," which can be observed in babies and small children. This reminds us of the saying of Jesus, "Unless you become as children, you cannot enter the Kingdom of Heaven."

Thus, the Taoist view on harmony does not carry moral overtones, as it refers to a state of being that is intrinsic in the body. This state of being of the body as a microcosm lies in the balance within and between its major organs, through which the body resonates with the energies and forces of the universe.

In the Taoist perception, there is no heaven or hell outside, above, or below us. They are seen as states of being of our bodies and our inner selves and the way we relate to the universe, ourselves, and one another. They reflect states of balance and imbalance between the positive and the negative. In this view, human beings are responsible for their own state of being, the quality of which depends on their self-awareness as the key to self-transformation.

This view is reflected in many ancient spiritual traditions and cultures which suggest that it is wiser to keep the devil as a friend than try to combat him and do away with him. This liberating view and its transformational force—which frees us from self-condemnation with its tendency to obscure the positive within the negative—is the basis for the Fusion practices.

LIFE AS AN INVITATION TO LEARNING

The Chinese character for crisis stands for both a problematic occurrence as well as for an opportunity, and this reflects the Taoist view of the unity of the positive and negative. In this perspective, whatever happens in life is to be seen as an invitation for learning and an opportunity for awakening. Theoretically speaking, problems are not really problems, but opportunities for self-transformation, since the negative contains the positive, in the same way as the positive contains the negative, like the yin in the yang, the yang in the yin. What you might see and experience as negative carries within it the seeds of the positive, just as the light exists within the dark. In this light, all the problems of life may be seen as energy potential, and as learning process.

This is a key premise in the Fusion practices, and it helps to overcome the duality we tend to construe, as a result of attachments to our negative experiences and emotions, thus keeping ourselves from entering into balance.

Taoists say that learning is enhanced if the organs feel at ease and find themselves in a state of well being. When a state of disease arises—which in Chinese medicine, of Taoist origin, is a symptom of the breakdown or weakening of the free flow of energy—learning becomes more difficult.

This state of mind also gives primacy to the need to reflect on your own attitude and perception in resolving problems; in other words, look inward to see in what way you have contributed to the problem and how you can contribute to its solution by changing your own attitude, perception, and way of life. Thus, from a Taoist perspective, problems are seen not as obstacles or difficulties but as opportunities to learn, and as learning material.

In this connection, it is interesting to note that the word *disaster*, common to many European languages, has its etymological root in the Latin substantive *astrum*, "star," of which it is a negation by the prefix *dis*. This suggests that originally, the word had the connotation that if and when one lost touch and became alienated from the stars (as representing our origins), one was in for trouble; imbalances would arise.

SMILING AS THE KEY TAOIST PRACTICE

Smiling and relaxation are the core practices of the Universal Tao. They are the key to the transformational process and to learning, as a result of which you are enabled to gently and patiently change old patterns into new, concerning yourself and the universe: new breathing, posture, inner and outer movement, and a new perception of reality.

Essential, therefore, in the Taoist practice to enhance learning and get in touch with the body by turning inward, is to learn to relax and smile inward. Doing so overcomes dis-ease, manifest in many forms of stress, and returns you to a state of ease. Thus it may be said that whereas the Western approach to medicine starts from outside, the Taoist approach starts from within.

It is not incidental that the whole practice of the Universal Tao starts with the practice of the Inner Smile. This is actually the first practice of Internal Alchemy, as it serves to soften our body and its elements, in which our consciousness is stored and through which it operates. It is the key agent of the whole activation and transformation process in all the practices. We do not only have a body but we also are our body. By touching it with love and gentleness, its knots and blockages start to dissolve so that the free flow of energy is restored.

THE UNITY OF
FULLNESS AND EMPTINESS

It is, in this context, not surprising that at the heart of the ancient Taoist texts is the emphasis on the practice of turning inward and of stillness. It follows that in the process of meditation, as a practice of becoming aware of the inner state of being of the body and its movements, we create a new and fresh space in which renewal and transformation can take place. This space is also called the creation of emptiness and the continuous re-creation of emptiness so that new fullness becomes possible.

In the Taoist as well as in the Buddhist traditions, which were closely related over long periods in Chinese history, emptiness and fullness are indivisible and a condition for each other. In the Universal Tao practices, this view has vast implications. For example, in the universe, emptiness and fullness are indivisible and are the creative source of becoming, evolving, and renewal, so that the universe is reborn in a continual process. We ourselves give thanks to the alternation of the inhale and the exhale, so our body is in a continuous process of dying and being reborn, through which we renew ourselves. The new can only arise when the old dissolves. So it is in Nature, with the change of seasons. And so it is with all that is alive in the universe. This is the core wisdom of the I Ching.

In the Taoist practice, this has a particular application in the counsel to empty the mind and let it come down in the body so that a major source of energy is preserved and can renew itself. At the same time, the belly can be filled with chi, so that the energy streams in the whole body are enhanced and the heart is freed from too much pressure, as

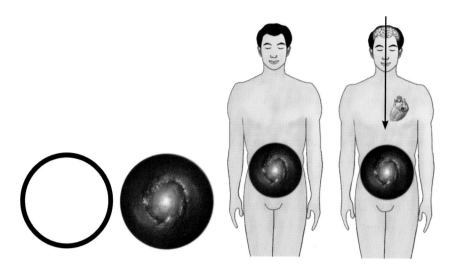

Fig. 9.3. The core is the center
of the universe, Earth, and the body.

the belly helps do its work. Only when we learn to renew ourselves by undoing what has become unnecessary and what obstructs the process of transformation do we renew ourselves and our body. By undoing in ourselves what is no longer needed, the new can grow. An ancient Taoist proverb suggests that simplicity comes about by seeing every day what has become dispensable. Then one can walk and move lightly, both in the mind and with the body.

Jesus often reminded people in his parables of the law of unity and alternation in nature, and of old and new in themselves. In the Tao Te Ching, this truth is expressed in rich metaphors, for example, the house that acquires its function by being empty and the wheel that receives its function by virtue of its emptiness.

The law of unity finds its most pregnant expression, however, in the unity of living and dying, an understanding common to all the great spiritual traditions—Hindu, Buddhist, and Christian—which is also central to Taoist practice. The new can only emerge and grow if the old dies and is discarded.

ATTACHMENT AND DETACHMENT

This insight is at the core of the I Ching, in which nature with its cycles and seasons is held up as a mirror for human beings. It has shaped from ancient times the Taoist proposition that to learn to be and to realize oneself, one needs to go with the flow of life and to become like a fish in the water or a cloud in the sky. This insight is essential to give depth to the Fusion practices: balance attachment with detachment.

In the Taoist view, attachment and detachment are not to be seen as opposites that exclude each other. What may be useful and functional in one stage of life, in one particular situation or moment, may

A: Why don't you sit down and relax. Let go of the weight and let me take you to the market.

B: Thank you for taking me to the market. I don't want to put too much weight on your car.

Fig. 9.4. Relax and let go.

well lose its functionality at another time. This explains why Taoists question the usefulness of externally induced and prearranged moral codes. Instead, they value, above all, self-cultivation in learning to act in harmony with what is inwardly experienced as genuine and truthful, because it is in tune with the universe in us.

The training in such an attitude, in which you free yourself from fixed rules imposed and determined from the outside, and consult your own body and inner feeling, creates both freedom and flexibility. It helps you avoid being trapped in positions that undermine the capacity to trust yourself, and at the same time it raises self-esteem.

In the process of genuine self-reflection and the growth of self-awareness, you learn to look at yourself and your inner life from a distance, and as a neutral witness, rather than as a judge. As a result, you grow into a spirit of inner freedom and you learn to look at yourself with a sense of relativity and even with a sense of humor. At the point you are able to truly smile at yourself and have reached the point you can forgive yourself, wisdom is dawning and the knots that you felt were blocking your way are in the process of dissolving, to create space for new and fresh energy.

GOING WITH THE FLOW

This view of going with the flow in the universe and within yourself is also the basic principle inspiring the ancient Taoist arts of self-defense. In Tai Chi, no position is fixed, and the body enters into a continuous flow of movements, as life is movement; and in the movement, to become one with the universe and its energies and forces, one becomes invulnerable. The power gained in the martial arts is not an external but an internal one, generated by the process of alignment. It is this alignment through which the body is empowered from below and above and the power can flow from the center.

If you have no center, you can be easily pushed around. A person who is centered has an internal balance. He or she is freer from external influences and less fearful and suspicious of others, more in tune with self and the universe. Therefore, the fusion practice may be called an internal kind of martial art by which practitioners learn to playfully bring into balance their opposites, so that a sense of being centered and in harmony arises and self-confidence manifests.

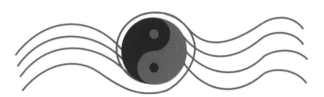

Fig. 9.5. Balanced, going with the flow

It should be obvious that the practice of these arts may be most helpful, as they may help you to remember to go with the flow inside yourself and become inwardly soft and flexible. Like all true Chi Kung—the art of moving the chi and moving with the chi—outer flexibility comes from inner relaxation. Only when relaxation deeply enters, can the body become truly receptive for the energy within and from outside. The same goes for Tai Chi.

The Fusion practices may also be seen as an inner play in which you invite your organs as your children to play with each other and see how they can balance and support each other. It may also be compared with an ancient game, which is played by children and adults in different countries of Asia. In Thailand, where it is called Takara, the players help each other in keeping the light bamboo ball in the air so that the play can continue. Nobody loses; nobody wins. Everybody gains: All share in the joy of the game and, in the process, gain in their own ability and help the others to enhance theirs.

Central in the Taoist tradition, the body expresses and balances both heaven and earth. How could it receive the energies of heaven and earth and become an expression of the universe, if it were not open and flexible and receptive? This explains the crucial role of Chi Kung and the various schools and forms created over the ages so as to make the body a vessel. As the Tao Te Ching says: the function of the vessel is to be empty so that it can be filled.

THE SECRET OF BREATHING AND RELAXATION

The essential role of breathing, in all the practices, is to enhance detoxification and cleansing, to create new space and openness toward the universe (in the exhale) and to fill the body with new energies and forces, by receiving, enriching, and transforming chi (the life or vital force). Breathing is central to the Taoist practice.

Changes in the quality of breathing from a short, superficial, and agitated breath in the upper part of the body to a long, deep, and quiet breath in the lower center/tan tien of the body are crucial to the process of inner transformation. This is because breathing is the bridge between consciousness and the body, and in the breathing process both the body and our awareness change.

The quality of breathing plays a crucial role in the processing and transforming of emotions. Key themes in the Fusion practices are the transformation of negative into positive emotions (Fusion of the Five Elements) and the cultivation of positive emotions (Cosmic Fusion). The emphasis in Taoist practice on self-healing is intimately related to the growth of self-awareness with regard to one's pattern of breathing, as this determines the ability to regulate, control, and balance emotions.

The Inner Smile practice as well as the Healing Sounds practice, designed to balance the negative and positive properties of the organs, are essential as preparation for the Fusion practices. It should now be clear that the practice of the Inner Smile and the quality of breathing and relaxation—as conditions of the self-healing process—are intimately related.

It is not a coincidence that the great sages and masters of self-transformation, like the Buddha and the Taoist immortals, are always portrayed with an inward-oriented smile, to signify the key to inner freedom and balance and the unity of yin and yang. The practice of the Inner Smile as the key to relaxation remains the basis of all the practices of the Universal Tao, from the most basic to the most advanced. It is the key to all forms and stages of self-transformation, as the Taoist masters discovered its secret and its power to initiate and enhance the process of self-transformation. Statues and pictures

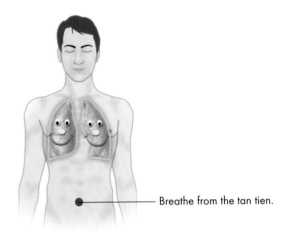

Breathe from the tan tien.

Fig. 9.6. Smile to the lungs.

may remind us of our own transformational potential and may help us to set in motion the internal alchemical process. We may also bring into our mind images of people who have awakened or who remind us of our own potential for transformation and our positive qualities, thereby helping us to empower ourselves.

THE SCIENCE OF FEELING AND THE POWER OF INTUITION

The Taoist practice is a continuous invitation to turn inward and get in touch with your own body (and organs). Begin to sense and feel the body's state of being, its expansion and contraction, and the relations between the major organs and the senses (kidneys/ears, liver/eyes, heart/tongue, spleen/mouth, and lungs/nose). Check the relationship between the major organs and connected organs (kidney/bladder, liver/gallbladder, heart/small intestine, spleen/stomach, lungs/large intestine). Review the overall state of relations between the organs, glands, the nervous system, the spine, the bones, muscles, and tendons. How are the relations between the three centers of the body (belly, heart, and Crystal Room)? Check on the relations between the center and the extremities, the front and the back; and check the quality of the paths, the routes that carry the flows in the body: the electromagnetic energy, called chi (also called the life force or vital force), the blood, and the lymph flows.

You can determine any advance in your practice by the growth in your ability to feel into the body by going inward and getting in touch with it.

In this context it is of value to realize that the verb *heal*, the substantive *whole*, and the adjective *holy* have the same etymological root. This is in line with the Taoist insight that the process of healing is realized in the process of becoming whole, and that holiness is the state of having become whole and in balance with oneself and with the universe within oneself. In this view, holiness is not a moral category but an existential and relational state of being.

It is not without reason that Taoist practice has been called a science of feeling, as throughout the ages it has relied on and cultivated feeling. The "power of intuition" is another way to describe the ability to feel, or you might call it the feeling intellect, which exists at all levels of our body and bodily awareness in which we are wholly present. All languages of the world contain a multitude of expressions referring to this capacity of the organs—the heart or the liver or the kidneys, the blood or the bones or the veins, the hands, eyes, ears, and feet—evidence of this intuitive power of the whole body. The association of thought with the mind and the brain only, so characteristic of Western reductionism, is entirely alien to all cultural traditions of the East and the South.

It is through feeling that we open the body and open and activate the chi from within and outside. It is also through feeling that we can sense, taste, hear, and touch the rhythms of earth and heaven and unite with them within ourselves. Becoming aware of our inner movements and of what moves us are one and the same thing. In the feeling process, we also become aware of the relativity of our boundaries and learn to experience these not only as limitations and finite but as openings to the unlimited and infinite.

As a result, our solitude comes to an end and we become sensitive to our intrinsic relatedness with all that is. In this sense, each practice may be seen as a step to invert the process toward alienation and separation from the sources of life, basic to Western culture and its extension over the world.

THINKING WITH THE HEART

Carl Gustav Jung, the famous Swiss psychiatrist and cultural philosopher in the 1920s, met with an old Pueblo Indian in New Mexico on one of his visits to the United States of America. Jung narrates in his autobiography that his talk with him was unlike any conversation he had ever had with a European. When Jung asked him how he felt about white people, Ochwia Biano (Mountain Lake) said that, to his people, they looked quite cruel in their appearance. "You always have an inflexible expression on your face. You always seem to be wanting something. You are always restless and agitated. We don't know what you want. You all seem to be quite crazy." Jung then asked him why he thought white people were crazy. He replied, "They say they think with their head." Jung, surprised, asked him, "Of course, but tell me, where do you think?" Ochwia Biano replied, "We think here." And he pointed to his heart. Jung tells how he sank into deep reflection. "For the first time in my life, it seemed to me, somebody had shown me the image of how we really are. . . . This Indian had touched our weak spot and pointed to something to which we are really blind." Jung viewed the encounter with the Indian as an opportunity that opened for him a new gate to a primordial and almost entirely forgotten dimension and form of consciousness, which could be revived.*

In another passage in his autobiography, Jung narrates a dream he had during a visit to an Islamic country in North Africa, which deeply touched him. In this dream, he had to fight for his survival with a young Arab aristocrat who descended from his horse and wanted to drown him. Jung interpreted the dream as a struggle between his own repressed unconscious (his shadow), which sought to be recognized

---

*C. G. Jung, *Memories, Dreams, Reflections*, ed. Aniela Jaffe, trans. Clara and Richard Winston (New York: Vintage, 1973).

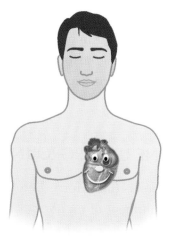

Fig. 9.7. Smile into the thinking, feeling heart.

and accepted, and his own consciousness, represented by his rational mind which felt threatened by the unsuspected attack by the young man. He then observes: "In my unconsciousness, I was in no way aware of such a situation; on the contrary I could not undo myself from a feeling of superiority, as at every step, I was reminded of being a European. I was not prepared to meet the unconscious forces within me, which emerged with such an intensity on behalf of the opposing party and which led to such an intense conflict."

Only several years later did Jung begin to understand the deeper nature of the dream. He began to see in the dream the resurgence of primordial structures or patterns in himself, from a well-known past, but a past he had forgotten. He perceived the resurgence of these images as a renewed awareness of a still-available potential for life overgrown by civilization, a potential for life that had been repressed and marginalized into the subconscious. In Jung's view, Western culture had become alienated from much of what being human represents: the primordial dimension of our being, which had been relegated to the underground.

Jung was a great admirer of the Taoist tradition and expressed his deep appreciation for its originality and wisdom in the foreword that he wrote for Wilhelm Reich's translation of the I Ching into German (the first translation of the I Ching into a European language).

The split between body and mind, thinking and feeling, matter and spirit, which is at the root of the formation of Western culture and religion and the birth of modern science, has been aggravated in the course of the twentieth century.

THE FEMININE UNDERGROUND CURRENT

Some historians and scholars (like Morris Berman in his path-breaking studies, "The Re-Enchantment of the World" and "Returning to Our Senses") have argued that in the course of this process of alienation, the feminine dimension of European culture greatly suffered, and in order to survive had to make itself invisible, and so became its undercurrent. He means by this that in religion, with its reliance on external authority and its contempt for the body, as well as in science, with its pursuit of mental objectivity at the expense of other sources of cognition, the body was devalued.

Subsequently, the body could be turned into a mere object, an input and an instrument. It was seen as a function of externally determined aims, as defined by the forces of competition, economic rationality, and rational management and the new communications technologies. This process has seriously undermined the position of women and has greatly affected their sense of dignity and self-esteem. It has also challenged the yin values in society, which are considered to be counterproductive.

Unquestionably, the growing sense of despair and disorientation experienced by large groups of people in the world today is directly related to the split and the resulting imbalances they experience within themselves.

RESTORING THE BALANCE

With the growth of a new world culture, with a process of unceasing economic expansion and the simultaneous rise of both minority affluence and mass poverty, these dualist tendencies are being further aggravated. We see the rise of fundamentalism and dogmatism, as instruments to legitimize power and achieve control, and as a response to a growing despair and an expression of the thirst for security. This is a further sign that the world, rocked by imbalances and social fluctuations, has become increasingly uncontrollable. The uncontrollability is seen as unavoidable and inherent in the very mechanics of the system and as an inevitable price for economic growth and "advancement."

Repression of the body and of sexuality and a search to compensate for it go hand in hand. Thus, both repression and a desperate search for liberation from it are both on the rise. There is a trend to see the body and sexuality as the source of all evil and to start crusades against them so as to secure law and order. There is at the same time a growing obsession to secure and maximize pleasure, a trend that is the object of ruthless exploitation in which the body and sexuality have become mere commodities on the market. Public life is being sexualized, as a source of economic expansion and profit.

Thus the repression of the body and sexuality has precisely an inverse effect, as a fast-growing market and rapidly expanding pleasure and amusement industry capitalizes on this repression.

The first law of thermodynamics states that energy cannot be created or destroyed. In terms of Taoist theory, all energy comes forth from the Great Void, the original Wu Chi, which undergoes a series of transformations in the formation of the universe. Thus the human body is seen as one particular form in the transformation of this original energy.

The second law of thermodynamics states that energy in a closed system tends to become disorganized (entropy). Thus there is an automatic tendency for balance to be lost. Taoist practice focuses on inverting the process of dispersion and disorganization and restoring balance. This process is set in motion and facilitated by the Healing Love practice, through which the unity and balance between love and sex is restored.

Essential to the Healing Love practice is the growth of love and compassion within, as a result of which love and compassion for others and the universe become possible and emerge as a natural extension. Once inner balance is restored, it is possible to act as an effective agent of outward balance.

In the Taoist view, conflict and violence in the outer order invariably have their source in inner conflict and violence, as manifestations of inner imbalance. Equally is outward peace viewed to have its source in inner peace and balance. In this process toward inner balance, Fusion practices, in conjunction with the Healing Love practice and other practices of the Universal Tao, play an essential role; they honor the body and its intrinsic wisdom and potential for self-healing and rebalancing, so that it enters into alignment with the universe.

Joseph Needham, one of the great scholars of the origins of Chinese science and civilization and an honored member of the Academia of Science, called Taoism the feminine undercurrent in Chinese history and culture, because of its focus on the power of silence, feeling, sensing, compassion, forgiveness, humility, gentleness, reverence for life and nature, and the equality of women.

It was, however, relegated to the margin of Chinese civilization and its practitioners often had to go underground. As a rule they fiercely stood for the ancient communitarian practices of reciprocity and sharing, as well as for the people's freedom and self-reliance. At the same time, they were opposed to interfering with the natural order, which was to be respected as a manifestation of the higher orders.

THE WORLD AS A MANIFESTATION AND REFLECTION OF THE UNIVERSE

The Taoists valued ancient forms of democratic practice, rooted in a vision of village communities in early times, which formed federations patterned on the very structure of and alignment with the cosmos. No wonder they were staunchly opposed to any form of feudal hierarchy in which undue power was exercised by the few over the many, and to the rise of a wealthy aristocracy that lived at the expense of the common people. They were also opposed to any form of technology that would harm nature or the people's sense of well-being. Their attitude toward the universe and toward each other is summarized in the words of Lao Tzu:

> *The universe is sacred*
> *You cannot improve it*
> *If you try to*
> *You will ruin it*
> *If you try to hold it*
> *You will lose it*
> *Surrender yourself humbly*
> *Then you can be trusted to take care of all things.*
> *Love the world as you love yourself;*
> *Then you can truly take care of all things.*

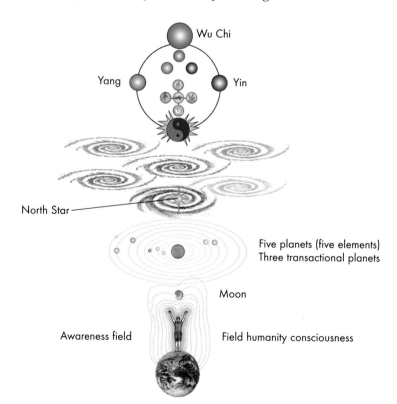

Fig. 9.8. Alignment of the cosmos

It may well be that, precisely because Taoist practitioners refused to be co-opted by the establishment and were relegated to a precarious position, the practices could survive. These practices, as presented in the Universal Tao, constitute a synthesis of several thousands of years of practice by generations of Taoist masters of the science of feeling and sensing inward and of observing the nature of the universe and our relations with it.

Their history provides evidence that Taoists over the centuries had a genuine concern about the well-being of the common people and that they found in their practice no reason to disengage from the world. The many stories and legends of the Immortals show that they were greatly loved, especially by the common people and the poor, whom they often protected and helped. Their practice of gentleness (kidney), of generosity (liver), love and respect (heart), fairness and openness (spleen) and courage (lungs) expressed a strong sense of compassion for those who suffered.

THE BODY AS THE PRIMARY SOURCE OF COGNITION

In the evolution of Western culture we see a progressive disconnection between body and mind, thinking and feeling, rationality and emotions, mind and energy, inner and outer, matter and energy, linearity and spontaneity. Feeling as a source of awareness and the primary mode of cognition has been progressively devalued. It was seen as a feminine value, of little use except in such domains as that of the arts and artistic endeavor. In religion, feeling as cognition was considered, together with the body, sexuality, and emotions, as a potential source of evil. In science with its drive for objectivity, it was also looked at with suspicion, as it tended to disturb and undermine the demands for objectivity.

Thus, cognitive feeling was relegated to an inferior position, as it was supposed to interfere with the rationality, discipline, and order needed for progress and the growth of modernity, as well as for the drive to control the universe, the cosmos, nature, and ourselves.

In the Taoist tradition, feeling as the power of intuition, rooted in the body, and the ability of self-reflection have always been considered the primary sources of self-awareness. Jung called this form of cognition the knowledge of the unconscious, a knowledge that underlies all conscious activity of the mind.

This capacity to intuit reality exists in our whole bodily being. The ability to sense reality in its totality may be called an integral form of knowledge. It may also be called a mode of thinking with the body that precedes all the formalized codes of thinking that evolved with the advance of formal rationality and the split of body and mind. In that sense, it may be called a yin form of cognition, as opposed to the yang form of cognition, which characterizes the modern world and its connected forms of education, science, and technology. Yet there is abundant evidence that at the source of all genuine creativity and inventiveness, including in the field of science, lies the power of intuition.

The Universal Tao and the Fusion practices, deeply rooted in the Taoist tradition, may be seen as a way to recover this form of knowledge within ourselves so that the split within ourselves between body and mind, feeling and thinking is overcome. In the great Asian traditions, thinking—in its restricted sense as the linear activity of the brain—has been viewed as interfering with and affecting awareness as the primary and principal form of knowledge, essential for turning knowledge into understanding.

From a Taoist perspective, the primary learning process does not take place in the brain but in the organs. Recent findings corroborate the Taoist vision of the learning process: that the brain only processes what is experienced and known intuitively by the organs, in particular those in the lower tan tien.

Our deep memory, which structures our patterns of reaction and response to the world, lies in the organs. In this view, a learning process needs to be rooted in a relearning and a reprogramming of our subconscious in the organs, from which all conscious activity springs. In terms of contemporary technology, the organs are the software and the brains are the hardware.

THE UNITY OF WHAT IS ABOVE AND BELOW

In many recent attempts to revitalize and recuperate spirituality, people have felt a growing need to counter the ominous trend toward a loss of meaning in the world. There is a tendency to continue the split that inspired spiritual traditions that tended to be based on the duality of good and evil, higher and lower.

As the lower part of the body and its organs has come to be associated with the instinctive, animal, obscure part, connected with sexuality, which obstructs the mind and the spirit in its upward vocation, it is ignored and bypassed. The Taoist approach fully honors and recuperates the dignity of the body as a whole. The Tao recognizes the belly and its organs, connected with our sexuality and water energy, the source of creative power from which all energy transformations flow. By getting in touch with our most intimate parts, we also gain access to the source of our creative powers.

The Fusion practices invite us to reconnect with those parts of ourselves, both physically and psychically, that have been the focus of repression. This repression is not only in most of our cultures but also within ourselves, as we have each internalized what we've learned in our culture, at home, in school, and though the media. In order to reconnect and truly get in touch with our organs, we need an instrument capable of understanding them.

That instrument is our intuitive power, which has its roots in our body as Earth. No other instrument can substitute for it—including our own intellect, through which we are often at risk to become strangers to our own innate wisdom.

Genuine self-transformation can only be realized from within by the one who truly knows her/his personal existential history. We must see the relations between positive and negative emotions as our own most intimate history, which we have often hidden from our own senses and which only reveals itself to our own compassionate inner eye and our own loving energy. Only then can we open the path to true healing from within. No medical system, medical doctor, psychologist, psychotherapist, or other professional can do what you

Fig. 9.9. As below, so above.

yourself can do: to observe and understand yourself emotionally and feel what your innermost self needs and longs for.

To this end, the Fusion practices are a primary means to reconnect with the somatic basis of our being and to reconnect with the hidden parts of ourselves. The Fusion practices are exercises in kinesthetic awareness through which we recover our primary form of knowledge, which is somatic and is buried in our very body and our gut. For this, we need to go deep down into our own emotional history and learn to feel with and within our entire body. For this, we need to let our rationalizing mind deeply sink into our body and let our intuition take over so that we get in touch with the visceral level of our being. Thus the Fusion practices are not mental or intellectual exercises to clear our debris or to accumulate virtues, but existential, transformational exercises to which the formal mind only becomes an impediment.

The Fusion practices provide a unique way to overcome the

dependencies we have grown accustomed to, to train ourselves in self-reliance, and to recover our independence and thereby our self-esteem.

HEALING WOUNDS

The question is asked: "Where to begin?" Such questions may suggest a hesitation to enter the practice and face oneself. A path opens at the very moment we start to walk. The inner journey is different for all of us, as our histories are unique. The formulas provide an essential guide, which tells us how to go, which direction to take, when to walk, when to rest, and what stations (practices and sequences) we should visit.

As suggested earlier, the whole Taoist practice has its beginning in the practice of the Inner Smile. The Inner Smile as the key to refresh, create, transform, attract, and blend energies presupposes a basic willingness to enter into an adventure and to face the risks in transforming old to new. It requires, above all, self-compassion and a willingness to love yourself. Such an inner movement toward the opening of the heart is only possible if you have some willingness to accept—and forgive—yourself.

Perhaps the primary key to any process of self-transformation is the willingness to forgive oneself, as it opens the heart and sets in motion and frees the flow of chi, both from within and without. That would seem a necessary condition for an open space to emerge, in which you can enter into dialogue with the organs, letting them speak and listening to what they wish to say.

Yet forgiveness is not a once-and-for-all act but a primary key in a continuous process of turning inward and practicing inner observation. It is not surprising that when Jesus was asked a question about forgiveness, he pointed to its key role by saying that a man should forgive seventy times seven, meaning that forgiveness has no limit. Rather than perceiving forgiveness as a virtue that makes possible all other virtues, like love and compassion, it is more useful to see it in terms of growth generated by the process toward a balance between positive and negative emotions (Fusion of the Five

Elements) and as the fruit of the creative cycle (Cosmic Fusion).

The refusal or inability to forgive and thereby to love oneself and others may be said to affect all the organs, affecting their chemistry and inhibiting cooperation and balance. Frequently it is rooted in a victim consciousness, which sets into motion negative emotions that tend to reinforce each other. This victim consciousness often has its roots in a presumption of betrayal, as a result of which the heart closes, as others are made accountable for one's own negativity and suffering.

As a result, the person refuses to even consider looking inward, as the source of misfortune is placed outward. Thus the heart's natural tendency toward love and compassion is obstructed, and the person cultivates the wound in order to legitimize his or her withdrawal from life. Both the internal flow as well as the inward flow from the outside are being impeded. All traumas first of all settle deeply in the organs, from where they affect the flow of energy. They can only be dissolved with patience and gentleness toward oneself. Only when internal energy is accumulating can it flow outward.

The strengthening of the organs has, in the Taoist tradition, a vital role to play in mitigating the negative emotions and achieving control over them. Forgiving does not mean that the wound needs to be closed. It may remain; but it is no longer active in generating toxins and does not prevent the growth of positive emotions. Also, forgiving does not means that you forget. That may be too difficult and is not necessary. Only the charge, which activates toxins, needs to be defused.

The aim of the Fusion practices is not to eliminate pain. Pain and joy are intrinsic in life and form a unity of opposites. Attempts to eliminate pain create frustration and exasperation and may well make it grow and become more difficult to control, as negative emotions such as fear, anger, worry, sadness, and impatience multiply. The more negative emotions are suppressed, the more they have a tendency to run wild.

The purpose of the Fusion practices is to achieve control and to regulate emotions consciously so that major imbalances can be prevented and the quality of the energies, upon being fused and blended, is heightened. Then transformations into new states of being (energy body and spirit body) become possible. Ups and downs are inevitable. But as you grow able to accept them and balance them, as you grow in equanimity, a point comes when you are less affected by what happens around you; you are less carried away by events, and you become less vulnerable.

Rather than doing away with toxins, it is wiser to allow for them and it is easier to control them. You raise immunity by balancing positive and negative emotions (Fusion of the Five Elements) and by strengthening the positive emotions (Cosmic Fusion). The unity of the two is of great importance. To make a small tree grow, you do not only weed, but you also ensure the optimal conditions for the tree to grow: that it is planted in good soil, that it receives shade and water, and that it is pruned at the right time.

One practical way to deal effectively with the negative emotions is to distinguish between them, so that you can separate and sort them, and give them the attention they require in order to become manageable. You might see them as your children who all have their specific needs. You can give to each one the particular attention it deserves. To deal with them all at once is too difficult and leads easily to discouragement and a sense of powerlessness and defeat. In an individual way you can work with them more easily.

For each of us, the relations among and between the positive and negative emotions is a unique one. So are our needs and styles to deal with them, depending on the culture we grew up in, our different kinds of education, and the ways we have responded and evolved. We will need to rely on our own imaginativeness to use the formulas creatively, so that they will help, rather than become an obstacle if we apply them mechanically. We need to learn to feel what is good for us and what helps us to be centered, in balance, and at peace with ourselves.

THE PRACTICE OF HUMOR
AND THE HUMOR OF PRACTICE

Crucial to our practice is a sense of humor and playfulness: to avoid the Fusion practice becoming a reproduction of old patterns in a new form, as we use it to track down our weaknesses in a spirit of self-condemnation. Humor is essential for balancing the energies of and in our organs. Humor is the great regulator, helping us to look with a sense of relativity, playfulness, and lightness at ourselves. It is an expression of the compassionate energy of the heart. Humor helps us to look with a sense of detachment at ourselves and not take ourselves so seriously that it becomes difficult to relax and witness rather than judge.

With little humor, Fusion would become an accounting practice, in which we record the drawbacks that prevent us from advancing. In judging the negative as if it were evil, we lose sight of our creative potential and prevent our gradually freeing ourselves from old patterns. Without humor, we see no way out except by relying on some external power or force, which only further undermines our own original power of self-transformation.

LEARNING TO TEND OUR GARDEN

What helps is to realize that we do not have negative emotions, per se, but that we and our spirit are in them. They are an integral part of us, and when we want to eradicate them, we destroy ourselves and the spirit contained in the organs.

For the Fusion practices to become effective, we need to learn to have a dialogue with our organs. We must learn to express our gratitude to them for the miracle of being alive thanks to their unceasing work. We need to give them a chance to relax and recuperate. Let us give them a chance to get in touch with each other. They are our children and our parents both. They can store chi and provide us with energy when we need it. Let us protect them from our anger and other negative emotions, so that they do not have to suffer and feel we drain them. Let them breathe freely, accumulate chi, expel the accumulated toxins so that we can recover, nourish, and sustain our health and vitality.

It is a challenge to see the positive in the negative; negative emotions, when freed from their destructive and explosive charge, contain pure energy which we badly need to develop our vital force.

To accept ourselves, it helps if we remember that our negative emotions often mirror forms of resistance that, at some time early in life, served as a form of legitimate and understandable protection and rebellion. At that long-ago moment they might have been necessary, but at some point they lose their function.

Negative energies may be seen as a kind of garbage. If we discharge them on others and the environment, they become a major factor in generating toxins, bacteria, viruses, and a variety of disease forms by which negative emotions are multiplied and become more and more difficult to control. Or, if we conserve and recycle them, they can be seen as highly positive and urgently needed for composting, so that they can help us grow and improve our balance. Then we become not a burden and a threat for others and our environment, but a blessing, as our energies contribute to a climate of harmony and peace. The more light and chi that enters our body and the more we radiate it into others and our surroundings, the less bacteria and viruses have a chance to grow.

The Fusion practice (Formula 4, Fusion of the Five Elements) provides an effective method for composting, as the negative energies from the different organs, after having been separated out in the collection points, are brought into the pakuas, which act as transformers. There, we can blend them with the positive energies from the organs as well as the energies from the universe, so that they become purified and enriched, generating energies of a higher quality and order. These we can then condense into a pearl as the embryo of our energy body (Formula 5, Fusion of the Five Elements).

RAISING THE QUALITY OF OUR ENERGIES

The Cosmic Fusion practices basically serve to consolidate, stabilize, and enhance the process toward balance initiated in the Fusion of the Five Elements practices. The Creative Cycle practice of Cosmic Fusion specifically serves to further the growth of positive energies in the organs and glands, which in turn will be able to mutually support each other to create a higher quality of energy. This energy is concentrated in the compassion energy from which we form a pearl. Only when all the positive energies merge into the fire of love and compassion by which the sexual energy is steamed and transformed, will its energy turn into a higher creative and spiritual energy. This higher energy will then serve to nourish the energy body.

This pearl will be more powerful in healing and cleansing the body than the pearl in the Cosmic Fusion practice and may subsequently serve to create and nourish the energy body. The energy body may in the highest practices give birth to the spirit body. The Cosmic Fusion practice also serves to intensify the process of cleansing and healing through the creation of the three Thrusting Channels and by creating the nine Belt Channels, which serve to protect the body and its energies from negative influences.

MARRIAGE OF THE LIGHT FROM WITHIN AND FROM ABOVE

All Universal Tao practices, including the Fusion practices, consist of two dimensions. One is the activity that focuses on the processes of transformation within the body through cleansing, opening, healing, and fortifying the body and raising the quality of its energies. The other dimension is to get in touch with the universe and nature and attract their energies and the Light in which they originate toward the body, so that the body may process these energies and blend them with its own refined energies.

The Taoist view is that the body, by its very nature and structure, is a microcosm, able to attract, receive, and use the energies from the universe, the cosmos, and nature to transform itself. Quantum physics confirms the view that the mind is faster than light and that consciousness is a form of energy that can move other energies when tuning into these energies and their frequencies. With its meridians, our body may be seen as a grid of light channels through which it is connected with the light grid of the universe and can tap its unlimited energies.

Fig. 9.10. Connecting with the universe

The process of getting in touch with the universe and expanding love and compassion begins in the same way as the approach to inward transformation of energy: with smiling, feeling and sensing, and radiating out love energy. The cleaner and finer the energy emitted, the higher the response from the forces and energies from above, below, and around us. The relationship with the universe has been likened to that of a love or courting relationship. In all the mystical traditions, the experience of the divine is also experienced as a relationship between the lover and the beloved. Frequently, the great mystics have expressed such relationships in the most erotic and sensuous language, another reason they were rarely accepted and often persecuted.

LEARNING TO EMBRACE OURSELVES AND THE UNIVERSE

The Fusion practice may help you to visualize yourself as a network of light and as a light body. Then the practice is not only one of cleansing but also one of filling the meridians with light. Mutations in consciousness start in the body visualization and turn into actualization. But the transformation lies not just in the visualization. That is only a vehicle. Actualization is the real experience of the energy transformation in the body, when its chemistry changes and energy is transformed. You begin to sense the truthfulness and miracle of being alive and you start to feel that you are embraced and pervaded by love, and a sense of gratitude for the mysterious ecstatic process taking place in the body arises.

But this is not an end term. It is always only a beginning, as the love of the infinite has no limits, neither in time nor space. In the process, matter turns into what is immaterial, and the immaterial, as energy continuing its transformation, looks again for a new form to contain it and change its nature and composition. Words help to create an image, and when the image is there, the word loses its function. The image serves to help us generate the energy and its transformation. When the energy has come into being, we need to give the image up so that a new space arises for a new experience. This is an unending process. How wondrous it is that our organs and our body—that sacred vessel, as it is called in the Taoist canon—remember their origins and longs to be fused and to serve as an instrument of the fusions that unceasingly occur in heaven, so that we can realize and experience our intrinsically divine nature.

For earthlings, the learning process starts from the outside. In the process of turning inward, the learning process increasingly becomes internalized. We need the structures and the forms and formulas to help us on our path. Then, when we become still, the process becomes spontaneous and starts to move by itself.

Then our children have been born and they just want to play without end, to feel that they are welcome and loved, to feel at home. For this quality in us to arise, we need to learn to embrace ourselves and the universe, as a mother her newborn child.

Appendix

Questions and Answers about the Cosmic Fusion Practice

Q. Is the cauldron the point where all the pakuas join together?

A. Yes.

Q. Now that we've learned about the cauldron, where do we collect the energy at the end of meditation practice?

A. You can collect and store energy at the cauldron or you can continue to collect and store your energy behind the navel. When you collect the energy you make a vortex, which is three-dimensional, so it can veer toward the navel or the cauldron. As you do this you may feel it going deeper and deeper.

Q. Do we always have to do 36 and 24 spirals in the collection?

A. The numbers 36 and 24 are a guide. There is no speed limit for spiraling the energy when you collect it. Some days you might want to do more than that; on many days you may want to do much less. On those days, 12 and 9 may be sufficient. Eventually it will go by itself.

Q. How do you collect the energy when there is so much energy all around?

A. Collecting the energy will eventually become automatic. The safety features are bringing any excess energy from the pelvis up to the navel and excess energy in the head and heart down to the navel. When you are coming back from the feet to the navel in the Belt Routes you are also collecting the energy.

Q. Does the energy stay in the cauldron or does it spread to the organs?

A. Both.

Q. Should you see the collection points in color?

A. Some people see, some people feel, and some people can even taste the energies. If you are visual, great. Then you will see the colors. If you work with the colors, the color will tell you if an organ's energy is healthy or not. If you look within and see dark muddy colors, then you know you have to work to make them clear and bright.

This applies to the organs and the collection points. Because the organs are affected by the emotions the colors will be affected.

Q. Does the yin/yang symbol move inside the pakua?

A. It spins like a vortex.

Q. Is there always a pearl you can work with?

A. If you practice forming a pearl every day, there will be one there when you sit down to meditate.

Q. Is there a minimum size for the pearl?

A. The size of the pearl is less important than its density. As you add energy to it you might notice it glowing more brightly or feeling more energetic.

When the energy increases, you might want to make more than one pearl. Then you can give it away to an organ or into your own atmosphere.

Q. Does the Belt Channel go around both legs or each one separately?

A. It circles around both legs, although if the energy wants to go around each one, that's okay too.

Q. You talk about using the Thrusting Routes for practical purposes. Can you give an example?

A. To clean the atmosphere in a room, you shoot the pearl out the crown and let it expand and fill the space. That way you declare the territory as your own—it is permeated now with your energy and consciousness. If there is any negative energy, any negative spirit, it will just leave of its own accord. You can't destroy negative energy, but you can work with it to make it leave, by overcoming it with your own energy. But you don't want to anger another spirit, that's not the Taoist way. Either they are using your energy to protect themselves or they want to tap into yours to get themselves to a higher level.

Q. Is there a breathing technique that will make you more yin or more yang?

A. It's not just breathing. If you eat very yang foods, like meat, and you are trying to be yin, it won't work. If you work with the Fusion I formula, you can balance the energy more easily than with outside forms of breathing or food. Fusion I and the Microcosmic Orbit are natural ways to balance your energy.

Q. The meditation seems so long.

A. Once the channels are open you don't need to spend much time. The training period seems long, but the actual practice can be quite short. When the Thrusting Channels are open you won't need to do any muscle contractions, you won't need to do it in stages, you won't need to inhale several times. You will just sit down and in a couple of minutes you will find yourself in a state where the energy will be strong enough and the channels open enough that the energy will flow through the Thrusting Channels just using the mind itself. In fact, you will be able to do it anytime, not just during meditation.

You can imagine the work it takes to connect pipes from a reservoir to each household in a city. But once the pipe is connected, all you have to do is turn the faucet on.

Q. What can close the channels?

A. Stress of any kind can close the channels. Tension contracts everything—muscles as well as emotions. Also, if you stop practicing for
a long time the channels will close. A path that's walked on every
day will be clear, but if no one travels on it the weeds start growing
and soon it is covered back over. That's why we stress the importance of daily practice. Even five minutes a day is better than one
hour once a week. Fusion I and Fusion II practice can be combined
together, so you can check the organs, smile down, see what you
need to do, and in a few minutes you can do some maintenance
work. Then when you have more time you can go and clean the
organs and the Thrusting Channels. In the beginning, the Fusion
practice needs the mind to form the pakuas and collection points.
It's like the Microcosmic Orbit: when you first learned it, it took a
lot of concentration on each point, and even when it started to run
by itself it wasn't dependable. But after a while you could wake up
in the morning and feel your Microcosmic Orbit running.

   Fusion I and II are more complex, and at the beginning you
have to develop a different technique to get them running. I
just look in the cauldron and it's like a slide projector: I can see
everything. Then you can add the collecting of the energy and the
blending process.

   Everyone we know who has practiced Fusion II for a year
or so, can do the Creation Cycle in a couple of minutes. As you
practice and keep adding more details, sooner or later it becomes
automatic. If you do Fusion II on a daily basis you will begin to
get faster and faster. You will be able to look inside and see what's
going on. When the process becomes automatic you open a whole
area of possibilities. It will give you more time to practice because
you will be doing it so fast. It will be there when you sink into
sleep. It will be there when you wake up in the morning.

   When you tune into your organs, your organs will have more
say over what they want and what they do. So when you work with
the formula correctly, the organs will love it. They will have the

space and time to be themselves. The brain can be overworked and pushed too hard. It can force any organ to work until it's destroyed. You can see this in people who take drugs to control their emotions.

But when the situation is balanced by using the Microcosmic Orbit, the organs get a chance to balance themselves. The brain has a say but the organ also has a say. Then you can achieve a balance of energy when the intellect and the organs are working together. At this stage, when the senses are drawn in, not distracted and running around, you will feel calm. Gathering and conserving energy is good in itself.

The next thing that happens is that you can begin to gain Real Knowledge. Real Knowledge is beyond intuition; it comes from within and you make better choices and decisions. This Real Knowledge is an inner guide that sometimes manifests in dreams from the unconscious. It can show you a direction in life. You know yourself that these dreams are rare. In the past they only came when you were at a crossroads and there was some danger. But through the practice with emotions, organs, and mind, you develop that interior communication that allows you access to Real Knowledge, so you're not operating in a state of emergency but from a state of balance and calm. Those directions will be easy to follow. So this is a process of purification. The energies will be used with purer intentions.

For example, if you have an excess of fear, you feel threatened and isolate yourself. Any decision you make from that standpoint will not lead to happiness. This formula is very important and carries a tremendous amount of responsibility, for whenever you learn something that can change your life in a positive sense you will either do it or forget about it. You often hear people say, "I want to change my karma." This formula is something that can change your karma. So this practice, this opportunity has a responsibility. You will have to take the consequences of doing it or not doing it. Because if you do it, you will change.

Q. How can I protect myself from negative energy?

A. The Belt Routes can protect you. When you circulate the energy through the Belt Routes, the energy centers are strengthened and can protect you from absorbing outside energy that you don't want. For instance, in a crowd, if there is energy you don't like, just run the Belt Routes to protect yourself. This will also protect your aura. If you are upset and have a lot of emotions, the aura is very unstable. The aura might expand or shrink. This protection will become automatic through diligent practice of the Belt Routes.

Q. When you send the energy out like a shower, are you always collecting positive energy? How do we know what energy we are collecting?

A. There is always heavenly energy around you, and there is always magnetism, so when you do this work you are working with earth and heaven energy. It's another responsibility when working with the energy. If you are an ordinary person you are absorbing only a certain level of energy. When you start raising your level, you are raising your level of positive energy. This can change the atmosphere around you (an inner pressure of positive energy). Energy has a magnetic quality that attracts. When you have strong positive pure energy, you will be repelling negative energy and you won't be affected by negative energy. For example, if someone is angry you will have enough positive energy to handle it. If you practice this and go to higher levels and then decide to stop, your pressure will again change and decrease. Our bodies always try to find a balance, that's our inner intelligence. So the pressure has dropped, and the body tries to restore the familiar higher pressure. To do this you start absorbing anything, and the most abundant source is the garbage energy: anger, fear, depression, etcetera. As you build up your strength you need to maintain that higher level, and that is a big responsibility.

So when you do the shower of energy you have to depend on the strength of the energy in your pearl. Fusion II jacks up the energy of the pearl you made in Fusion I by imbuing it with the positive qualities in the organs. So it's important to do Fusion I carefully.

When you absorb positive energy you can even affect the bacteria in the air. If you've been practicing the Microcosmic Orbit and Fusion I for a year, you've probably noticed that colds don't last as long, and you don't get sick as often.

Q. Is it normal to feel pain or discomfort when doing the Fusion practices?

A. You can see that some systems are into suffering: staring at the sun, sticking oneself with needles, or standing on one leg for a long time. This is so that when practitioners get to the level of great power, they can withstand the pain. This is how some people learn and they suffer a great deal.

Maybe you cannot take all the energy; some people bathe in the river every day to reduce the heat and can't sleep for weeks and months. When you practice to a certain level there are changes in the body—but you can take those changes. Sometimes as new energy pushes through channels you may feel a headache. Some people feel a stomach cramp when they blend the energy at the cauldron. But that is unusual. It's like trying to help a butterfly when it's hatching. Maybe you want to help by cutting the chrysalis with a scissors. But the butterfly won't survive if you do that. It has to struggle at the beginning in order to survive.

So you will have to grow over the pain. Other systems induce the suffering first. In Chinese, they call it *qing ku*—you don't have anything and you still have to suffer—but that is not the Taoist way. We prefer to grow first and then experience the growing pains. You may feel imbalanced from time to time—constipation is a real problem. If you have a good bowel movement at least once a day, you will not suffer so much.

Now that you are more sensitive to energy, you will recognize negative energy right away and you have the tools to neutralize and purify the energy.

Some people, after they study, find that they are reacting differently to their love partners. For some of them, this difference leads to a break-up. When they look back on it, they often realize that the break-up was inevitable and that they were dissatisfied before. For others, especially couples who study together, their relationship becomes more solid and more respectful. In any case, it means that you begin to understand yourself better.

Sometimes you begin to see problems more clearly and see the energy that causes the problems. When you can enhance the energy inside, the problem goes away. There are those who get angry but don't realize they are angry and aren't aware of the effect of the anger on the liver. But those who practice Fusion I can become aware of the liver and very quickly the anger will be gone.

The Taoist system can change the course of your life, change your astrology, change your fortune and your fate. We know that because of the experiences of Taoists over many generations.

The energy inside your organs and brain makes your life what it is. So when you know how to control your energy, your organs and senses, that is the beginning of controlling your future. Those who are controlled by substances like tobacco, alcohol, and other drugs are not in control of their lives.

In Taoism you don't run away from problems as long as you are in this world. Actually there is practically nowhere on the planet where you can go without being bothered.

When we started to teach Westerners, we found new ways to teach people how to balance their energy through diet as well as through the Taoist exercises. Those who eat only raw foods will be too yin and those who eat mostly meat and dairy will be too yang. But the only way to restore your Real Knowledge is when you turn to your internal organs and senses for information. Then you will know how to conduct your life. But until you do that, it's hard to know what's good or bad for you.

The golden mean, the middle, moderation are all ways of saying that when you know how nature works you will know the Tao.

By knowing the Tao you start to know about God and the universe. Anything that's extreme, you have to back away from. The only thing that lasts long is balanced, middle and center.

Q. Is there a problem if I shake a lot during meditation?

A. Too much shaking can scatter the energy. Moving and stillness have to be balanced. If you remain still for too long the energy might settle. But if you shake and scream and are never still you risk eventually shaking out all your life force.

  If you start burning a fire, it gets hotter and hotter. When the water comes to a boiling point you turn it down and cook it very slowly. That way you can get the essence out. If you don't turn down the light, all the water will boil away and the pot will be burnt or broken.

  When you are into the meditation and very still, movement starts, and many things are activated. If the movement becomes very strong it won't last long and you might want to stop it. You have to know the timing. If you start to shake, you can gain power by stopping the shaking and utilizing that energy inside. If you let the shaking continue, you might lose all the energy you built up.

  In some forms of therapy people are encouraged to shake and jump and scream to get rid of their anger or depression or anxiety. When the session is over it seems that everything has been worked out but when they get home they are thoroughly exhausted. The emotions were shaken out along with the life force. How much better to recycle the energy.

  Tai Chi balances the yin and yang through movement and stillness. This builds up energy and then you can circulate the energy in the Microcosmic Orbit. The whole secret in the Universal Tao is having the channel for the energy to flow.

Q. Why do you create an energy body outside yourself?

A. When you set up the energy body and the spirit body, they start to draw out the essence of the physical body. Then it starts to work in space.

It's the same reason that every country wants to set up laboratories in space. You can make a lot of things better in space because there's no gravity, no dust, and no germs.

The energy body will draw the essence up; you might even feel like it's going to pull your whole body up. And then the energy body draws the energy from space and the universe and mixes them in. When you bring the energy back into the body, the organs will absorb all this energy and start to transform. But if you sit down without a purpose you won't get this effect.

Every time you add more of your body's energy to the energy body, the energy body will go higher. Sometimes I feel like all my essence leaves my physical body. When you practice every day it starts to take the essence of this body and transform and mix it with the universal energy and your progress will be remarkable. There will be no resistance. When you're finished meditating, you just shrink the energy body down and each time you shrink it down the pearl becomes more refined.

At one time, the Taoist masters were afraid of losing the pearl in space and did it all inside the body. This was reflected in the art in China where they worked incredible detail on miniature objects. But later the Tao masters discovered that if they know how to send the energy out the head, they can expand the energy body and then shrink it down. That way they achieved more perfection—it's the same way they make a computer chip.

If you look inside a chip there's a whole city inside it. They draw every detail on paper the size of a football field and then with a special camera they shrink it down and down.

Set it up, do all the detail you want, then shrink it down and pull it back in.

I had to figure a lot of this out myself. When I heard "transfer your consciousness to the next life" I decided I had to learn how to do this in this lifetime. I kept asking, but everyone had a different answer. They just said it's very simple. I told one master I'd give him anything for the secret; I'd go anywhere to learn. Either he didn't have it or else he wouldn't give it to me. After a while I discovered that I'd have to figure out myself how to transfer whatever I wanted to the energy body. I did this because I understood that my energy body will live forever.

Focusing on intellectual understanding alone is limiting and stifling. A real practice teaches one how to feel within and derive authentic knowledge based on personal experience. In the Universal Tao, we emphasize the practice of understanding nature, getting in touch with the natural forces, and getting in touch with oneself. Then the principles of philosophy will reveal themselves, and one can have real hope based on what *is*, not on empty promises that can never be proven.

Bibliography

Beinfield, Harriet, L.Ac., and Efrem Korngold, L.Ac. *Between Heaven and Earth*. New York: Ballantine Books, 1991.

Grazzaniga, Michael S. *Nature's Mind*. New York: Basic Books, 1992.

Grings, William, and Michael Dawson. *Emotions and Bodily Responses: A Psychophysiological Approach*. New York: Academic Press, 1978.

Haas, Elson, M.D. *Staying Healthy with the Seasons*. Berkeley, Calif.: Celestial Arts, 1981.

Hammer, Leon, M.D. *Dragon Rises, Red Bird Flies*. Barrytown, N.Y.: Station Hill Press, 1990.

Herrmann, Ned. "How the Brain Works . . . and How to Help It Work Better." *Bottom Line Personal*, November 15, 1992, 9–10.

Locke, Steven, M.D. "How to Use Your Mind to Improve Your Health." *Bottom Line Personal*, August 30, 1992, 11–12.

Melchizedek, Drunvalo. *Ancient Secret of the Flower Life*, vols. I and II. Flagstaff, Ariz.: Light Technology Publishing, 1998, 2000.

Porush, David. "Finding God in the Three Pound Universe: The Neuroscience of Transcendence." *Omni*, October, 1993, 60–70.

Wagner, Bruce. "You Only Live Twice." *Details*, March 1994, 166–71, 213–319.

Tortora, Gerard J., and Sandra Reynolds Grabowski. *Introduction to the Human Body*. 5th ed. New York: John Wiley & Sons, 2001.

———. *Principles of Anatomy & Physiology*. 9th ed. New York: John Wiley & Sons, 2000.

About the Author

Mantak Chia has been studying the Taoist approach to life since childhood. His mastery of this ancient knowledge, enhanced by his study of other disciplines, has resulted in the development of the Universal Tao system, which is now being taught throughout the world.

Mantak Chia was born in Thailand to Chinese parents in 1944. When he was six years old, he learned from Buddhist monks how to sit and "still the mind." While in grammar school he learned traditional Thai boxing, and soon he went on to acquire considerable skill in Aikido, Yoga, and Tai Chi. His studies of the Taoist way of life began in earnest when he was a student in Hong Kong, ultimately leading to his mastery of a wide variety of esoteric disciplines. To better understand the mechanisms behind healing energy, he also studied Western anatomy and medical sciences.

Master Chia has taught his system of healing and energizing practices to tens of thousands of students and has trained more than two thousand instructors and practitioners throughout the world. He has established centers for Taoist study and training in many countries around the globe. In June 1990 he was honored by the International Congress of Chinese Medicine and Qi Gong (Chi Kung), which named him the Qi Gong Master of the Year.

The Universal Tao System and Training Center

THE UNIVERSAL TAO SYSTEM

The ultimate goal of Taoist practice is to transcend physical boundaries through the development of the soul and the spirit within the human. That is also the guiding principle behind the Universal Tao, a practical system of self-development that enables individuals to complete the harmonious evolution of their physical, mental, and spiritual bodies. Through a series of ancient Chinese meditative and internal energy exercises, the practitioner learns to increase physical energy, release tension, improve health, practice self-defense, and gain the ability to heal him- or herself and others. In the process of creating a solid foundation of health and well-being in the physical body, the practitioner also creates the basis for developing his or her spiritual potential by learning to tap into the natural energies of the sun, moon, earth, stars, and other environmental forces.

The Universal Tao practices are derived from ancient techniques rooted in the processes of nature. They have been gathered and integrated into a coherent, accessible system for well-being that works directly with the life force, or chi, that flows through the meridian system of the body.

Master Chia has spent years developing and perfecting techniques for teaching these traditional practices to students around the world through ongoing classes, workshops, private instruction, and healing sessions, as well as books and video and audio products. Further information can be obtained at www.universaltao.com.

THE UNIVERSAL TAO TRAINING CENTER

The Tao Garden Resort and Training Center in northern Thailand is the home of Master Chia and serves as the worldwide headquarters for Universal Tao activities. This integrated wellness, holistic health, and training center is situated on eighty acres surrounded by the beautiful Himalayan foothills near the historic walled city of Chiang Mai. The serene setting includes flower and herb gardens ideal for meditation, open-air pavilions for practicing Chi Kung, and a health and fitness spa.

The center offers classes year-round, as well as summer and winter retreats. It can accommodate two hundred students, and group leasing can be arranged. For information worldwide on courses, books, products, and other resources, see below:

RESOURCES

Universal Healing Tao Center
274 Moo 7, Luang Nua, Doi Saket, Chiang Mai, 50220 Thailand
Tel: (66)(53) 495-596 Fax: (66)(53) 495-852
E-mail: universaltao@universal-tao.com
Web site: www.universal-tao.com

For information on retreats and the health spa, contact:

Tao Garden Health Spa & Resort
E-mail: info@tao-garden.com, taogarden@hotmail.com
Web site: www.tao-garden.com

Good Chi • Good Heart • Good Intention

 # Index

vehicle, forming of, 187–88
virtues, 8–9, 29, 96
void. *See* Wu Chi

warming up, for meditation, 38–39
water element, 20. *See also* kan
wind. *See* sun
wood element, 20
world, 226–28

wounds, healing of, 232–34
Wu Chi, 12, 17–19, *18*
    return to, *23*
    stages of return to, 22–25

Yan, Martin F., 48
yang, 14, *18*, 18–19, 200–201, *209*, 242
yin, *18*, 18–19, 200–201, *209*, 242
Yung Chuan, 40

BOOKS OF RELATED INTEREST

Fusion of the Five Elements
Meditations for Transforming Negative Emotions
by Mantak Chia

Energy Balance through the Tao
Exercises for Cultivating Yin Energy
by Mantak Chia

Sexual Reflexology
Activating the Taoist Points of Love
by Mantak Chia and William U. Wei

Taoist Cosmic Healing
Chi Kung Color Healing Principles for
Detoxification and Rejuvenation
by Mantak Chia

Taoist Astral Healing
Chi Kung Healing Practices Using Star and Planet Energies
by Mantak Chia and Dirk Oellibrandt

Chi Nei Tsang
Chi Massage for the Vital Organs
by Mantak Chia

The Inner Structure of Tai Chi
Mastering the Classic Forms of Tai Chi Chi Kung
by Mantak Chia and Juan Li

The Secret Teachings of the Tao Te Ching
by Mantak Chia and Tao Huang

Inner Traditions • Bear & Company
P.O. Box 388
Rochester, VT 05767
1-800-246-8648
www.InnerTraditions.com

Or contact your local bookseller